MARCELLO DI MUZIO

FROM THE UNIVERSE TO THE SOUL

High spiritual teachings for a new consciousness

Copyright © 2021 by Marcello Di Muzio

First edition January 2021

Originally published in Italy as
Dall'Universo all'anima © by I Libri del Casato, Rome, in 2019

E-mail: marcellodimuzio2@gmail.com
ISBN 979-85-986-77-3-77
Cover: Rinaldo Maria Chiesa
Translation by: Susan Scott

Contents

Introduction   5

PART ONE
MAN

Prologue to Part One	9
The path of evolution	10
Evolution of the conscience	12
Know thyself	16
The spiritual snares of the ego	21
The birth of the ego	25
The ego is not the conscience	27
Human freedom	31
Will	43
Happiness	45
Karma	48
Pain	56
Reincarnation	61
Passing on	67
Life in the afterworld	80
The fable of Abdus	85
The Absolute	88

PART TWO
THE COSMOS

Prologue to Part Two	92
The planes of existence	93
The physical plane	95
The etheric plane	97
The astral plane	103

The mental plane	106
The akashic plane (the conscience)	108
Critique of classical evolutionism	110
The expanding Earth	113
The Sun	119
Life on other planets and extraterrestrials	121
Matter and vibration	129
The creation of matter and cymatics	134
Gravity	139
Electricity and magnetism	145
Conclusion	149
Acknowledgements	152
Bibliography and photo credits	153

Introduction

This book is about human beings. It speaks of what is around them, what moves them. Whoever is familiar with the writings of the *Florence Circle 77* and the *Ifior Circle* knows what I am talking about. But even more, the book is a distillation of a great many other sources and in-depth studies that aim to open the minds of those who seek logical, consistent, and comprehensible answers.

The book is not a summary of topics already known, but a progressive presentation of considerations, reflections, and expansions on a theme, often offered for the first time, in a reasoned exposition that may intrigue readers who are new to the subject as well as those already well-versed in it. My intention here is to take readers by the hand and accompany them in the discovery of reality as a mirror of ourselves, to examine the world and our inner being with new eyes.

Those familiar with the topics will find here excellent starting points for going more deeply into them and numerous new and innovative observations. Those who are new to this have nothing to worry about: the topics are always developed with the clearest, most practical simplicity. My constant aim is to explain, using simple words, something that is a new point of view outside the human dimension, discussing scientific, philosophical, and moral subjects with the modesty of practicality.

The effect of this approach is a pleasant, fluid reading experience, devoid of formulas and panegyrics, in which the simple – but always logical – exposition of the meaning renders understanding of it easy and accessible.

Let me make one thing clear: the book's purpose is not to convince anyone or lead them to "believe". I think information should only convey logic and cohesion and should be able to fit into a larger discourse, to establish a connection with empirical evidence when possible, and never to come into contradiction with itself.

It is absurd to think that the reader can believe a report which, no matter how logical, has to be convincing. Believing is always wrong. Life itself does not demand to believe, but to experience. And I am not writing at all to convince, but to stimulate a search.

So let us not think we can convince anyone other than ourselves.

Freedom of thought is the essence of being human; believing is our own error, trying to convince is error on the part of others. Believing is a conviction that paralyzes freedom and makes one rigid and dogmatic.

This book has the sole intent of stimulating the search for the self, in the attempt to shake us out of the cultural crystallization that enwraps people today.

Because, while it is legitimate to seek, before accepting a new concept we are duty-bound to ask ourselves if everything fits into a discourse that is logical, coherent, consistent, lasting, and devoid of contradictions. "To doubt everything, or to believe everything: here are two equally convenient solutions, since both of them dispense us from reflecting", the mathematician and physicist Henri Poincaré suggests. To reflect is the only thing that life asks us to do.

The topics treated here take their cue in part – but only in part – from the invaluable work done by the Guides of the Florence Circle 77 in Florence and the Ifior Circle in Genoa. They are the most innovative, logical and consistent available today among the spiritual messages that have reached us.

I decided to include some original narrative passages – printed in italics – for the purpose of enabling readers to get an idea of the illuminating caliber of the source.

Each topic discussed always includes the sources from which it draws origin and inspiration.

The first part of the book focuses on the individual, on its inner world and its journey in relation to the material and spiritual world. In a crescendo of pragmatic revelations, we discuss moral, philosophical, and spiritual concepts; we evaluate the relation between our own ego and the conscience and examine freedom and happiness, previous lives, and what awaits us in the practical life of the next world.

The second part discusses new frontiers of understanding the dynamics that move the universe and offers a clear and revolutionary, because innovative, vision of the physical reality that surrounds us.

We shall travel through matter, to then, bit by bit, lift the veil on the dimension of the afterworld. We discover that the matter of the astral plane has a characteristic that intrigues even the most superficial reader: it can be molded by the simple impulse of will and desire.

We shall engage in a dialogue – with disarming simplicity – on topics like matter, aura and prana, gravity, and electromagnetism. We discover unexpected curious facts about Earth and the Sun and give merited attention to the dynamics of UFOs and the inhabitants of other planets.

The topics unfold, always vividly capturing the reader's curiosity.

In closing, let me leave you with the words of the Guides of the Ifior Circle:

In the midst of the proliferation of spiritual associations – each one with its own fund of promises to attract other people – we do not promise you anything, because we do not have anything concrete to offer you: if you seek power over other creatures, do not listen to our words because you will not receive from them any power, any authority, any elevation; if you seek proof of the existence of a God, whoever He might be, you would be better off observing what surrounds you, because you will much more easily feel the certainty of His presence in a blade of grass than in a still, small voice; if you seek to feel proud, advanced, farther along in the journey, then move away from us, because we speak for everybody and not only for a few, not only for those who, it is thought, might understand better what we say.

In this perspective, read – O sons and daughters – what is written and do not mistake, as often, too often, one does, the messenger for the message. No matter how different the course of a river might look compared to others, it always ends up merging into the same ocean.[1]

Happy reading!

Marcello Di Muzio

---

[1] Ifior Circle, *Sussurri nel vento*, Genoa, Ins-Edit, 1991, pp. 13-14.

PART ONE
MAN

Prologue to Part One

The first part of this book lays out fundamental truths. It observes the human person in his own reflection.

The goal is to lead readers into an attentive inner journey, with the intent of revealing how conscience comes to be and what dynamics move the ego.

We shall find that the famous phrase *"know thyself"* is not only an exhortation for personal development, but above all the practical instrument available to us for moving forward in life and in evolution – to which each person is called – with the least possible suffering.

We shall explore the afterworld in minute detail and describe the mechanism that governs the cycles of reincarnation; we give freedom and will their proper role in the choices we make every day and redefine the purpose and meaning of existence.

The exposition of this multitude of new and innovative concepts finds its ultimate aim in the yearning to stimulate the search for our inner being *since – and we shall never tire of repeating this – the first step towards understanding the All proceeds from an understanding of ourselves.*[2]

So let's take things in order, above all slowly and patiently.

---

[2] Ifior Circle, *Dall'Uno all'Uno*, Genoa, Ins-Edit, 2011, vol. III, part I, p. 29.

The path of evolution

The first truth that every spiritual teaching aims to emphasize as it unfolds is that we should not identify ourselves only as our physical body. This material body is merely the dwelling place for a spiritual being. Beyond the physical plane, reality unfolds on other, more rarefied planes of existence that are not tangible to human beings as long as we remain immersed in material reality.

Just as on the physical plane individuals live through their physical body, for every other plane of existence they have an analogous vehicle. Thus it is not the brain that is the site of thought, but the individual's mental body. The origin of emotions is not chemical reactions, but the astral body.

Life, in order to manifest itself, needs to use various bodies, each one residing in a different dimension from the others. The human being is in reality a multidimensional being.

Each time a person lives, he possesses and manages various bodies, each one residing in a different dimensional plane:

- the *physical body*   which permits us to live in matter;
- the *etheric body*   the seat of energy to enable the physical body to live and to stay healthy;
- the *astral body*   which makes us feel emotions and desires;
- the *mental body*   the place where thoughts, reasoning, and memory reside.

These four bodies are already present at the moment of birth and are recreated each time a human being is reincarnated on Earth.

They are, ultimately, the bases – like containers – that predispose an individual to create his or her character, personality, physicality, and way of thinking, acting, and reacting to life.

All together, they constitute what we call the person's I, or ego. Above and beyond these four planes of existence is an individual's conscience. A person's conscience – that part which pushes him or her to make altruistic choices – is formed and increases every time an individual lives and assimilates new experiences on Earth. Sometimes the experiences are pleasant, other times painful; thus, each time, experience by experience, lifetime by lifetime, the conscience grows, evolves, is refined and enriched more and more. The person's understanding and sensitivity to other people increase, and he becomes more aware of the reality around him.

The purpose of life is the *evolution of the conscience*. Reincarnation is the means; that is to say, the individual, through multiple successive incarnations, by becoming saturated with the numerous and various experiences he has during his lifetime, ends up creating and expanding his conscience.

Conscience is truly defined as the sum of experiences. We can define life as the school of the conscience, where bit by bit the true maturity of evolved human beings is constructed.

The physical body thus acquires its new guise of a *vehicle of learning*, a garment that is worn for a certain period and then set aside. One enters this body in order to learn the most important of all lessons: *to know oneself*.

On the basis of what we said at the beginning, that a person is not identified solely by their physical body, it is easy to understand that when the physical body dies, a person in reality does not perish but, no longer having the physical vehicle that permits him to live on the physical plane, he transfers his awareness of living onto the astral plane – the one immediately after – where he experiences a new phase of existence. This is the Beyond that awaits us after we pass on.

This brief but necessary summary prepares us for reading the next chapters.

Evolution of the conscience

What is the conscience? Today, even science attempts to give us an answer. There is the profound conviction that the conscience is not created by the brain, that it is not simply the result of chemical processes in the brain. Physics even tries to identify conscience as the "unified field."[3] Historically, too, all the functions that are prerogatives of the mind or conscience have been considered as expressions of the word "soul". Conscience, Darwin wrote, is one of the "forces originally breathed by the Creator."[4]

A person's conscience corresponds to what psychoanalysis calls the super-ego.[5] In other words, it corresponds to the complex of moral rules that the individual has achieved in his various incarnations. It is an inner richness that will never be lost, given that evolution can never turn back, and the conscience, once acquired, constitutes the base for a new, higher level.

By evolution of the conscience we mean the individual's passage in time from a state of no conscience to a state of conscience, in other words from a state of the absence of a conscience to a state of a broader and broader conscience.

---

[3] A term coined by quantum physics to describe a theory that would unify all the fundamental interactions of nature.

[4] While in the original edition of 1859 Darwin did not mention the Creator, in later editions he added in the next-to-last sentence of *The Origin of Species*: "Therefore I should infer that probably all the organic beings which have ever lived on this earth have descended from some one primordial form, into which life was first breathed by the Creator" (Bert Thompson, Ph.D., *The Origin Of Species and Darwin's Reference to "the Creator,"* Montgomery, Apologetics Press, 2003).

[5] According to Freudian theory, the term super-ego indicates the ensemble of behavioral models, prohibitions, and orders and represents a hypothetical ideal towards which the person aims with his conduct. The super-ego is the representative of the highest ethical and moral ideals held by human beings. "It is a sort of censor who judges man's acts and desires" (Sergio Moravia, *Filosofia*, Florence, Le Monnier, 1999).

As humans evolve, they form their conscience, in other words they gradually acquire the inner maturity that, once achieved, makes them persons for whom morality is no longer an attitude imposed on them by external factors.

As we shall see in detail, the course of human evolution goes from the birth of self-awareness – the awareness that we exist – with the consequent rise of egoism, to the constitution of the individual conscience, that is to say, the overcoming of this egoism. The formation of this conscience is thus the purpose and goal of our continuing reincarnated rebirths.

In this sense, spiritual evolution can be expressed as the *sum of experiences* acquired over time, in our current incarnation and in the preceding ones. *Man embraces ideals and devotes himself to this. It does not matter whether they are right and just or not or if they correspond to the shared ethic; they are his ideals and in varying measure he lives for these. From this, he has different experiences, on the basis of which he adjusts his ideals and his life.*[6]

So, for human beings, evolving spiritually means that the conscience moves from minimum to maximum; it means that our moral ideal changes as the emergence of new experiences makes us understand the limits of an earlier way of thinking and acting. And in this way, as soon as a moral ideal is reached, slowly a new moral goal proposes itself to us, a new level of conscience, on which every individual sooner or later is called to reflect, through others' experiences or directly through their own.

Let us suppose, for example, that an individual spends his whole life as a miser. In a later incarnation, as a reaction he will in all probability be reborn as the victim of a person who makes him experience the same miserliness that characterized him in his earlier life. After an entire life spent experiencing the same conditions that he had imposed on others, he will have learned not to be stingy any more, but he will not have overcome the more subtle desires that lurked behind his miserliness. The miserliness, then, did not arise only from wanting to keep everything for himself, but also from wanting to appear to be greater than other people.

To satisfy this strong desire, the individual will live another life in which he will be a rich and famous personage, one who is so

---

[6] Florence Circle 77, *Oltre l'illusione*, Rome, Mediterranee, 1978, p. 253.

prodigal with his wealth as to show off to his audience. As a reaction, yet another life will be necessary for this individual to overcome the desire to show off.

In this way, from one experience to the next, from one lifetime to the next, people are forced to rethink their positions constantly. Science, too, teaches us that *every seven years the human body, by dint of renewing every day the cells that have worn out, has completely changed. So then, our hands, our face at a minimum are not the same as seven years ago.*[7]

This is why we must not denigrate someone who is still at a lower level of evolution, because *"a flower that has not yet bloomed is not to be condemned." Here is why God's justice would be inconceivable without His mercy.*[8] This is why Christ said so often not to judge others.

Even the most enlightened of saints has always achieved a heightened conscience through earlier experiences, the same ones as those of primitive people, which first taught them the basic foundations of life, then led them to understand through a certain way of reasoning, and then carried them to that higher level of feeling. Always – let's keep that in mind.

To be sure, talking about the evolution of human beings in a historical moment like this one means running the risk of not being believed because, in effect, hearing about current events and looking around us, it seems that humankind has not only not progressed, but has actually reversed direction and is going backwards.

Let us hypothesize that Earth is a school – and it is, given that it serves precisely to impart evolution to its inhabitants just as a school serves to impart instruction to its pupils. *If someone looks at a school from the outside, without realizing who the individuals are who attend it, they will say: "The years go by and these students don't learn anything – they are always in school!" Similarly, looking from the outside, one could say: "These people never evolve!" But the fact is that they are not the same people, just as it is not always the same pupils attending that same school.*[9]

---

[7] *Ibid.*, p. 256.
[8] Florence Circle 77, *Dai mondi invisibili*, Rome, Mediterranee, 1977, p. 236.
[9] Florence Circle 77, *Le Grandi verità ricercate dall'uomo*, Rome, Mediterranee, 1982, p. 162.

By this we mean that when the individual conscience has reached a level such that it is no longer necessary or useful to continue to be reincarnated in the physical plane, on Earth, its place will be taken by other consciences, which will have to begin their formative process from the very beginning, in the same way as a new pupil in that school.

To sum up, given that the ultimate aim of life is the evolution of the conscience – from zero to the maximum that planet Earth can provide – we can deduce that what human beings must pay attention to in the course of their lives is everything that in some way determines an increase in the conscience. This should not be expressed in extremist attitudes like abandoning everything and giving oneself up to the meditative life but, on the contrary, we are asked only to make a more aware reflection about ourselves and the repercussions this has on society as the environment in which we are immersed.

In the next chapters we shall see various themes unfold, which will engage the individual on the topic of achieving the evolution of the conscience, the key goal of life.

Know thyself

"*Know thyself.*" We all are aware that this exhortation has accompanied the human journey for millennia. And in fact, as many people know, it was inscribed on the temple at Delphi in ancient Greece.[10]

Through the centuries, many have taken "know thyself" as a dogma, as something that a person has to do in order to achieve something, but this is not the case. The meaning of this teaching is quite different.

"Know thyself" is simply the indication of the path that every individual – willingly or not – has perforce to cover in their life in order to reach the state of understanding, of inner awareness that will enable them to understand the mechanisms of existence and above all to reduce life's painful experiences. Otherwise they will continue to be knocked about from one experience to the next until life manages to breach their defenses and to bring them, whether they want to or not, the understandings that they cannot succeed in achieving otherwise.

Evolution will take place in any case and in no matter what condition the individual finds himself, but "know thyself" will save him, in a word, from the most painful experiences to achieve this. "Know thyself" means knowing the true reality of our being. It means understanding what in us comes from our environment and the outside forces that condition us.

By living continuously immersed in a social and cultural environment, a person inevitably receives from it a certain amount of influence. There is nothing wrong with this. The individual's error, if anything, lies in believing that upbringing, the formation of his or her character, can derive exclusively from outside factors.

---

[10] The exhortation "Know thyself" (*gnōthi sautón*) is an ancient Greek maxim engraved on the temple of Apollo, the seat of Delphic oracular knowledge.

Knowing oneself means, then, carrying out attentive, sincere introspection. It means understanding, for example, if what we believe to be patience, altruism, or love really is that.

It means knowing our desires, our convictions, our reactions to situations. Knowing them not because they must be morally judged and corrected – knowing them means simply knowing about them, being aware of them as if we were observing the behavior of another person, nothing more.

To be sure, it is not enough to think we can just set ourselves down somewhere and, all of a sudden, expect to know ourselves. Self-knowledge must be conquered. It must be discovered slowly and constantly along the course of one's life, together with all those elements and clues that can contribute or help to make it possible, truer, deeper. Knowing oneself means, in the last analysis, reaching the point of knowing one's limits. Moral limits, limits of character or way of thinking, limits of patience, limits coming from preconceptions, limits in giving, and so on.

So defend yourselves from your fellow man if, after a sincere examination of yourselves, you discover that you do not have the strength to put up with another's offense; stand up to those who want to take away your tunic if you do not truly have the generosity to give them your cloak too. An act of altruism carried out without evaluating its weight and consequences is a gift that you make without knowing what you have given; it is an IOU that you do not know if you will be able to pay back. Knowing your limits means this.[11]

Know your limits precisely in order to avoid setting in motion causes that in the future could have painful repercussions.

If an individual, even while living a comfortable life, wanted at all costs to earn and possess more than a coworker, in the event that he didn't succeed he could very well justify his "failure" by blaming economic circumstances or adverse events that came up which kept him from achieving a higher salary; however, his suffering could be avoided in large part by understanding that, in reality, what is suffering is not the physical person but his ego, which felt belittled and uncomfortable in relation to his other colleagues who have more.

---

[11] Florence Circle 77, *Conosci te stesso?*, Rome, Mediterranee, 1990, p. 94.

Without the awareness of who we are and what moves us, our ego (in other words ourselves at a level of unawareness) will create a thousand excuses to hide its egoism, for the sole purpose of building itself up.

Being self-aware does not mean assuming the guise of the ego in order to analyze oneself, but finding the strength to place oneself *outside* the ego, observing its actions and reactions *as if this were another person*. All for the sole purpose of understanding – precisely as if we were judging another person – what really drives us to act in one way rather than another.

For this intent to succeed, the fundamental attribute is sincerity with yourselves, which is difficult to keep constant but absolutely necessary in order to escape the more or less subtle traps that the ego places along your path for the purpose of knocking you off-course.[12]

Luckily, life offers us two valuable allies to help us in this exercise: our everyday experience, which continually offers us numerous chances to know ourselves better, and the experience of others; and we are by now submerged by moral cues on which to reflect and compare views.

It is clear that at the base of every person's existence there is egoism and that egoism cannot be uprooted ipso facto.[13] Already in a person's first incarnation, egoism is born with him. Realizing that he exists and not having other means for working out a balanced reaction to the outside world and to others, not yet having an established conscience – from the evolutive standpoint he is naked – he reacts in the manner that for his level of moral logic seems simplest, that is to say by exploiting the environment, thus also his neighbor, for his own greatest benefit. The self-centered ego will prevail in every decision and will make up the dominant character of the individual in the course of that lifetime.

But how is it possible to overcome the self-centered ego? For centuries, when people thought about this problem, spurred on by the great spiritualities, they believed it was enough to act like altruists to cancel out their egoism, and they never thought instead that, even though changing the external attitude, the inner nature

---

[12] Ifior Circle, *Dall'Uno all'Uno, op. cit.*, vol. II, part I, pp. 84-90.
[13] Florence Circle 77, *Dai mondi invisibili*, Rome, Mediterranee, 1977, p.85, par.1.

remains unchanged. It is perfectly useless for an ambitious person to sprinkle his head with ashes if he has not changed his inner nature; he will do it undoubtedly in order to merit a prominent place in a supposed spiritual life.[14]

By this we do not mean to say that imitating a higher morality has no benefit at all. Indeed, behaving in a more just, more upright way towards our fellow men has extremely important value for the society in which we live. But we have to keep firmly in mind that this is not sufficient to lead us to change. Inside, in moments of need, we go back to being what we were before. Nonetheless, doing our duty towards our neighbor is necessary and fundamental so that individual freedom does not become egotistical arrogance and abuse of power towards others. It is, shall we say, the first step.

You see, you can call the purpose of human life whatever you like, but – in essence – it means only one thing: to overcome a self-centered view of existence.[15] This, in a nutshell, is the purpose of a person's life. So then, what should we do? Once again, all that is needed is a bit of perseverance and a lot of patience. That is to say, it is necessary to carry out a sort of self-psychoanalysis, as though in our everyday life we were always in front of a mirror.

We must pay attention to our state of mind, our behavior, our habits, and especially to our reactions. Once again, we have to be as good at judging ourselves as we are at judging others.

"Why did he ask me this question?" "Why did he react in that way?" Now we have to ask these same questions of ourselves, maintaining the same emotional detachment and the same keen sincerity of judgment that we have towards others.

Let's try another example. Let us suppose that, as we analyze ourselves, we discover that we are social climbers who do not hesitate to climb over someone, especially our coworkers, to reach our goals so as to make ourselves look better and to be "more" than others. First of all, ambition, from a certain point of view, is not a fault but a virtue because it makes a person more active; it is a creative stimulus that pushes people to try out ever new things.

But if ambition, as presented in the example, is created on the basis of egoism and is thus damaging for others, the individual

---

[14] *Ibid.*, p. 85, paragraph 2.
[15] *Ibid.*, paragraph 3.

becomes a slave to his own ego and cruel towards his fellow men. *So then, ambition is a fault that should be rooted out at the source, and we reach the root not by acting unambitious, but by placing ourselves outside the conception that leads us to be overambitious.*[16]

This means that it is not by denying ourselves and forcing ourselves not to be overambitious that we will improve our inner being; it is certainly a praiseworthy gesture towards others to restrain the egotistical attitudes that we discover in ourselves, and this is certainly the first step to take in the right direction.

But we must also understand that this is the result of a merely exterior attitude. Even after making these gestures we shall not be changed in our innermost being; it will be only a new awareness that happiness does not lie in accumulating things and roles or being more than others that will bring about this true change of conscience. Only then will extreme ambition, as we have described it, not interest us any more.

This is what is meant by "know yourself." It is not easy – anything but. It is a long labor, as long as an entire lifetime.

The alternative for us is to let life take over in everything, strong in the certainty that life will take care of it, with its more or less painful experiences putting us back on the path ordained for our evolution.

---

[16] Florence Circle 77, *La voce dell'ignoto*, Rome, Mediterranee, 1983, p. 48.

The spiritual snares of the ego

The spiritual path of human beings is a fertile terrain, where the ego always weaves those subtle processes by which it realizes its ambitious plots, to the point of camouflaging and masking absolutely egotistical intentions with attitudes that can even be altruistic.

The most immediate example is in religions and all those spiritual disciplines in which adepts, in what seems like humble devotion of their life to God, are meanwhile focusing on earning a prominent position in the Kingdom of Heaven. This is a widespread attitude, and there is absolutely nothing shameful about this behavior.

"The conscience is never mistaken; if anything, it is insufficient,"[17] we are often told. This incomprehension is generated by the ego, which always seeks out the most ambitious path so as to put itself in the best light.

Today's world is pervaded by a multitude of splendid spiritual disciplines that teach people to meditate and exercise self-control, to relax the mind and body, to become aware of their reactions. *The disciplines are useful and should be followed to the extent that they limit themselves to promising only all that. When, instead, they promise progress on the path of the spirit or, even worse, the artificial acquisition of paranormal powers, then they become harmful.*[18]

In the same way, it is clear that whoever pursues these disciplines in the hope of these promises might do so because, urged on by their ambitious ego, they would like, for example, to stand out in a society in which maybe they have not been able to emerge in any other way.

If this is the case, once again, they do it only to boost their ego,

---

[17] Florence Circle 77, *Maestro, perché?*, Rome, Mediterranee, 1985, p. 71.
[18] Florence Circle 77, *Le Grandi verità ricercate dall'uomo*, p. 60.

and they would not have made one single step in the direction of the evolution they had hoped, in that their conscience, their innermost understanding, would remain unchanged.

The truth of a person is *intention*. The action of an individual in and of itself is only a set of movements devoid of moral meaning unless it is evaluated from the standpoint of why the action was carried out. Then, viewed under the lens of intent, every action can change its meaning. *A person is known by his intentions; if the intent is egotistical, the individual is egotistic, even if he is intent on carrying out a highly humanitarian act.*[19]

Therefore, it is perfectly useless to modify one's external conduct, one's "guise", when the intention remains the same.

Not even giving up all one's desires is a plausible path in terms of evolution, in that believing that happiness can arise and be maintained only in the absence of desire is an error of self-evaluation. *Then man seeks to dominate himself, to repress his instincts, to become the master of himself. As we have said repeatedly, a self-discipline of this sort is praiseworthy when it has the intent of improving relations among people. Unfortunately, the self-discipline which a person imposes on himself in this phase of his existence does not have the altruistic intent of improving human relations, but the egotistical intent of achieving an ideal of a "superman", therefore a happy one, gratified by his own superiority.*[20]

Some spiritual disciplines, unfortunately, encourage this perspective: in essence they admit that the reason for human suffering is the self-centered ego, but they do not seek a way of overcoming it, but rather evade it by concealing it with elevation of the hidden desire for spiritual superiority.

Instead of finding a way to tamp it down, they sublimate it by hiding it behind showy altruistic gestures or adorning it with an ostensibly heightened spiritual life.

According to this perspective, human beings are capable of making great sacrifices; they can give up spontaneously what others seek and long for, but the reason for their renunciation is the same as the one that pushes others to accumulate. In each of these

---

[19] Florence Circle 77, *Per un mondo migliore*, Rome, Mediterranee, 1981, p. 29.
[20] *Ibid.*, p. 41.

attitudes, what one aims to achieve is the affirmation of one's ego in this world or the next.[21]

Even an ascetic life is never preferable when isolation represents the suffering individual's flight from the stimuli of the environment and society.

The proper position, then, of a person who believes in a spiritual meaning for life is not one that leads him to isolate himself, to withdraw from the world; it is one in which the contemplative life is conceived, at most, as a transitional phase, a pause for reflection, because it is precisely from contact with one's fellow men and with the most disparate situations that the necessary stimuli for broadening one's conscience are received.[22]

In the same way, each of us is called to act, not isolated from the world but in the society and environment in which we live.

If we find ourselves living in a given environment, clearly it is to provoke a reaction in us, to stimulate us in certain experiences rather than in others. Before deciding to abandon everything that surrounds us and to look elsewhere in the search for ourselves, it would not be a bad idea to reflect that perhaps we ought to begin right where we are.

How? *By starting small and from close by*, say the Guides.

Start with simple gestures towards our family, our friends, those who are around us. *In moments of enthusiasm we would like to bring peace to the world, but before this we must look inside ourselves to see if we are at peace with our neighbors; this is where we have to start. We will not repent, certainly, for the great things that we did not do because we could not do them, but the little things that we neglected.*[23]

We must understand that the ego, if on one hand it is the necessary and irreplaceable support that sustains us and enables us to go forward in the choices we make in life, on the other it is the illusion that we must place under observation in order to move beyond it when it is no longer necessary and is starting to limit us in our relations with our fellow men. Then, after all the experiences that have helped us mature, we discover that a desire we once would

---

[21] *Loc. cit.*
[22] Florence Circle 77, *Le Grandi verità ricercate dall'uomo*, p. 81.
[23] Florence Circle 77, *Conosci te stesso?*, p. 15.

have loved to satisfy becomes almost a bother, a residual burden we must shake off, as if, in some way, it were blocking us on our journey.

The ego is the necessary ladder we have to climb if we want to evolve, because our ego is the only support we have, from which we must start out in order to move, consciously and unconsciously, between one experience and another.

Thus, between success and disappointment, joy and failure, satisfaction and pain, a person progresses towards the misunderstandings that, once they are remedied by experience, will become acquired conscience. This new level of conscience will never be lost and will form the base from which the new ego will start out to move towards new experiences.

And we shall obtain the awareness of what moves us in everyday life only by making this intimate effort to know ourselves.

Because each one of us – in short – is responsible for the world in which we live in the degree to which we do or don't do anything to change ourselves.

The birth of the ego

What is the origin of this ego which limits us so much? The ego, we have seen, is born when the person is born. In their first incarnations, individuals are conscious only of themselves. They have not accumulated many experiences and possess no other measure of judgment than themselves. *At this point it is easy to understand that for the individual a new world opens up: the world of I. Thus the individual knows deeply and perceives deeply egoism, greed, the urge to possess: stimuli that arise from the ego, from feeling separate from what surrounds us. This self-centeredness is initially violent and manifests itself in violent forms: theft, murder, violence, because the individual* (in that phase) *is not too different from an animal, and seeks the shortest path possible to come into possession of the object of his desire.*[24]

So then, there need to be factors that make it possible to limit this violent action of the individual in order to wreak the least damage possible on the others around him. Limits that work on him internally, like taboos and phobias, and externally, like laws and moral and religious commandments which, under the threat of punishment or restriction of freedom, keep him from carrying out certain violent acts.

Therefore, at this level of evolution, social and religious institutions are necessary and fundamental for the individual, not so much for the formation of his conscience as above all to set in motion the necessary limitation of his freedom of will.

Much later, when the individual's evolution and thus his spiritual maturity are such that he not only would never commit, but would never even conceive of these acts of egotistical violence, only then do the religious organizations and rules *in primis* lose their significance and purpose for him.

But egoism, note well, was up to that moment of evolution the

---

[24] Florence Circle 77, *Per un mondo migliore*, p. 119.

thrust that propelled it forward, that enabled this multiplicity of experiences, from the satisfaction of the coarsest desires all the way up to their relative consequences – first and foremost, suffering and dissatisfaction – enabling him, between one blow and another, to develop his astral and mental bodies (vehicles of the individual present in every incarnation) in an adult manner and permitting him to feel emotions and thoughts that are more sensitive and mature.

Satisfying one's needs (or at least trying to do so) means going so far as to consider oneself to be the pivot around which all of reality revolves so that (and how often, unfortunately) the needs of others become irrelevant, if not even a motive for a struggle for supremacy. Seeing the world as a function of oneself means tending to consider one's own needs so important that all of reality seems to have to converge on one sole purpose: to satisfy them. Consequently, whenever these people encounter other individuals who inevitably oppose this egocentrism with their own, this gives rise to frustrations, aggressive reactions, the attempt to prevail over or dominate the other.[25]

To summarize briefly: the ego – it is important to understand this – is a natural mechanism, whose birth is tied indissolubly to the individual's becoming aware of itself, to the point that its manifestation in a human being is not only inevitable but is the indispensable means for forming a conscience.

The ego is the indispensable companion on the journey which will lead the individual, by degrees, to emerge from the chain of reincarnation. There comes a moment, in fact, when the individual has to realize that the ego must be gradually abandoned, just as we let go of aids for walking, because from that moment the person has become an adult from the standpoint of evolution. Egoism, at this point, no longer has any reason to exist.

---

[25] Ifior Circle, *Dall'Uno all'Uno*, vol. I, p. 70.

The ego is not the conscience

In light of what has been said, one might erroneously think that the ego is nothing other than our conscience at a still insufficient state, as though *the conscience were closely dependent on the sense of self, to the point that there is no conscience without a sense of self.*[26] This view is completely mistaken. The ego manifests itself where the conscience is still lacking.

We can compare the evolution of the conscience to a container. In the beginning of the series of incarnations the container is empty, and the empty part is the person's ego. Bit by bit, as experience by experience the conscience begins to fill the container, the ego diminishes and begins to vanish.

The ego is in essence the illusory and transitory part that is "created" each time, in each incarnation, precisely for the purpose of enabling the person to have the experiences that will enable him to transcend the egocentric ego itself.

A person, ultimately, uses his ego to learn to get rid of it.

The ego manifests itself in an individual as his personality, his character, his way of thinking and acting, and his physical and emotional characteristics.

The ego is nothing other than the result of the sum of the astral (emotional reactions and desires), mental (thought and reasoning) and physical (body type and physical traits) bodies which, interacting with each other, experience the material plane for the purpose of having evolutionary experiences.

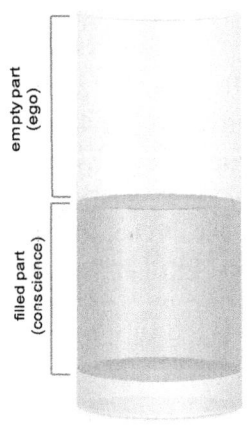

Fig. 1 - The evolution of the conscience is like a container to be filled

---

[26] Florence Circle 77, *Le Grandi verità ricercate dall'uomo*, p. 115.

It is not true that the individual conscience comes forth when the ego is gone, but precisely the opposite is the case: bit by bit, as the individual conscience takes shape, the ego is overcome.

This is an important concept to understand. In other words, we must not believe, as people mistakenly do, that by repressing thoughts, desires, and selfish actions a person broadens his conscience; this is a mistake, and this fact must be emphasized. Repressing leads a person to a form of alienation of life, to living in a world that is not real, to behaving in a phony manner with others and being false with oneself. All this is nothing more than wanting to shine in others' eyes, to fool oneself and others.

It is always praiseworthy to behave in a correct and altruistic manner, and this is the duty that each person is called to perform towards society. But towards ourselves, this is not even minimally sufficient, and in the long run forcing things in this way leads only to behavioral imbalances that will sooner or later find an outlet in other weaknesses. A person must dig deep and bring to the surface the true nature of his actions, the true mover behind his egoism.

Tom feels, for instance, a strong desire to have what Dick has, and to improve himself he convinces himself that he must absolutely repress his envy. Maybe he does it because – on an unconscious level – this way he will look better than Dick in others' eyes.

But what is repressed does not go away; rather, it continues to act on an unconscious level. Everything that is repressed resurfaces. Desire is not eliminated but only hidden from our awareness. *Desire is ego,* and the ego disappears only when it is replaced, in that aspect, by the conscience acquired. Up until then, this envious desire will take different forms, manifesting itself under other aspects, and Tom will draw the necessary experiences from those other aspects.

It is a bit like proceeding to solve a problem through *reductio ad absurdum*, or proof by absurdity, by following longer, and often opposing, paths. Tom, it should be well understood, will evolve just the same and in the same measure no matter what path he takes. He will reach in any case an understanding of what he is missing for overcoming envy, whether he takes the path of "know thyself" and tries to correct himself voluntarily or follows his desires and emotions, letting himself be swept along by the current of whatever happens to him in life.

But in the *economy of the individual,* he could save himself some time and above all some suffering. Because following each time one's own desires or giving – quite rightly – one's emotions free rein, but without having observed them or placed them in doubt, is like passively and constantly giving in to a spoiled child.

For our ego is like that child; and if we are its parent we have the duty, at the very least, to listen and be present to him.

In a nutshell then, what do we have to do? Once again, we only have to make ourselves aware that the ego exists because the conscience is not there yet, and thus to accept our egoism, seeking only to observe it in all its breadth of action.

What, we don't have to do anything? Exactly. Or rather: we don't have to do anything other than observe constantly in order to judge ourselves as if we were judging someone else. Like a sort of *therapy of self-psychoanalysis.* That's all.

The ego should not be repressed but brought out into the open. When we discover ourselves to be selfish it makes no sense to force ourselves into an altruism that we don't feel, because this would lead us to wear a mask that sooner or later we would pay for with a sense of dissatisfaction, depression, or release in other spheres.

Observation and sincere judgment, we have said, never repression. But if it is true that we must not repress, it is also true that we must not let the ego manifest itself freely, giving in and wallowing each time as it suits us in a wait for something to improve. If we do this, life sooner or later will present the bill for our egotistical actions, manifesting, just as a cause moves its effects, the corrective experience, which will be painful for us.

And our suffering will be greater the more resistance our ego opposes, consciously or unconsciously, in reaction to that painful experience.

Then we will discover that the ego should be watched constantly and attentively for the sole purpose of having all the information necessary to be able to decide with certainty how and when to let it manifest itself, but choosing what we could call the *path of least resistance.*

Why resistance? Because the ego, each time that in a situation it chooses the same solution which is egotistically most convenient for it, does nothing other than clog the "filter" of understanding. It is like filling the drain of a sink with sand. The more sand we put in, the more it will act as a filter, increasingly obstructing the flow of water.

The *filter* is the resistance that the ego has accumulated over time. In other words, it will correspond to the suffering that a person will undergo to remove it. Because the time will come when the filter will be too much and the conscience will not find any other way to get rid of the sand obstructing it than to remove it by force. Something unexpected, then, will happen in the person's life that will force him to an understanding; the painful correction will take place. The experience will come that will make him suffer.

The ego, we know, is always strengthened by habit; but comfortable, convenient, egoistical habit puts up a resistance to change. And this opposition is stronger the more deeply rooted the habit in us that causes the accumulation of *filter* and greater future suffering.

The *path of least resistance* corresponds to the voluntary choice in which the individual, choosing in a different and a little more altruistic way, decides of his own free will to accept a small blow, like a minor suffering that he does not find unbearable.

This voluntary choice, but of a very slight suffering – such as a small sacrifice – is, among the many choices that we could made in that given moment, a choice that is a little more altruistic than is our normal habit; but at the same time, this will be a choice that tends to minimize the suffering ego, to the point of perceiving it at most as a bother. Because any more than that, we could not bear it.

In a moment of anger, for example, it is as if we chose to control ourselves a tiny bit more than usual, at the limit of our tolerance, which is not the same as repressing ourselves; we must act without trying to force the limits of our tolerance.

It is as though the individual made a qualitative leap in terms of choice. *Know thyself* then takes on a whole new value: It is the tool that enables us to make a bit more conscious choices, which enables us thus to take away a little of the sand that has built up.

In this way, choice by choice, a person decides whether to continue accumulating or to start getting rid of the sand that clogs the filter of understanding.

A person's freedom of choice, as we shall see in the next chapter, is just this: to decide each time, grain by grain, whether to continue to accumulate or to start to remove.

Evolution of the conscience, in short, is made concrete in these little choices. And the only instrument we have to achieve our aim is to observe ourselves constantly in our actions, reactions, and relations of everyday life.

Human freedom

"Presupposing free will, every human reason would be an unexplainable miracle, an effect without a cause," Schopenhauer rightly observed.[27]

Determining to what extent a person is free has always been an impassioned debate. "I am free if I can do as I please," is the key concept of freedom.

But human beings, immersed in the physical world, are subject to time and space, and the law of cause and effect is valid both for objects and for the causes that drive their actions.

If a person seen *from inside* – that is from his own point of view – is actually free in his choices simply because there is no forcing involved, that same person *seen from the outside* might appear driven in his choices by something other than just his own will. In other words, if we could evaluate his choices seeing them from above, if we could see his life going by as a whole, we would probably realize that his choices are conditioned at times by a preconception, other times influenced by the surrounding environment, so that, even though the individual decides of his own free will, this will seems at the very least to be "guided."

Up to what point do outside conditionings influence choices? Up to what point is free will truly uncoupled from any form of determinism?

How much of a person is free of the chain of relations between cause and effect that unequivocally binds the material world?

Maybe Leibniz was right with his idea of "spiritual automaton" when he stated that man is like a machine that is so complicated as to seem to be free: the fact, in other words, of not being able to know the determination of everything gives us the illusion of freedom.[28]

---

[27] See Arthur Schopenhauer, *On the Freedom of the Will*, translated by Eric J. Payne, Cambridge, Cambridge University Press, 1999.

Let's try to see freedom from another point of view, that of actual life: A man commits a crime, and nothing kept that man from choosing not to do it. If human beings, as opposed to animals, have the capacity at least to *think* about alternative choices in order to avoid or provoke an event, this is all we need for now to state that this person, in some way, has free will. "So far as a man thinks, he is free," Ralph Waldo Emerson suggests to us.[29]

The question of free will became a pressing one for man when religion placed man in front of *full* freedom of choice between good and evil, between redemption and damnation. The concept of *absolute* free will is blatantly unsuited and unrealistic and by now is maintained only by Catholic theology. The fact that we do not enjoy free will is obvious to everybody. *By the very fact of having a physical body, for example, human beings are necessarily subjected to influences and necessities, and cannot be free in an absolute sense.*

So then, the account to be reckoned is that of relative freedom; that is to say, a person is certainly influenced, certainly undergoes influences that come from his environment, his own personality, the upbringing he was given, however in some ways he has the possibility of avoiding those influences.[30]

These final words – "the possibility of avoiding those influences" – give rise to a new nuance of freedom: it is a more pragmatic freedom, more *subtle* if you will.

Let us take an example: a man comes home tired after work. Maybe he would like to stay home and rest in front of the TV, but his wife really wants to go out to the movies. So here the choice delineates two different qualities of freedom: a rougher, more general freedom, dictated by – note carefully – legitimate physical needs, and a more subtle freedom, given by an altruistic form of reasoning, suggested by a greater sensitivity on the part of the individual, who acts only for his wife's happiness and, setting aside his tiredness, yields to her wish.

---

[28] See *Theodicy: Essays on the Goodness of God, the Freedom on Man and the Origin of Evil*. Translated by E. M. Huggard. La Salle, IL, Open Court, 1985.
[29] Ralph Waldo Emerson, *The Conduct of Life*, Boston, Fireside Editions, 1909, p.27.
[30] Florence Circle 77, *Maestro, perché?*, p. 93, par. 2

Choosing the first alternative entails a physical type of deterministic chain: since he is tired, he would prefer to stay home and rest. However, *another deterministic chain worms its way into this physical deterministic chain, a psychological one: his wife would like to go out, and so he, to make her happy, does not yield to his tiredness but suppresses it and goes out.* [31]

On the level of the evolution of the person's conscience, it is as though, while the first choice will always produce effects in the material world, the second will yield effects in the spiritual world. It is as though in the second case a "qualitative leap" takes place between these deterministic chains, and it is possible, through these leaps, to escape the choices that, even though made with a premise of freedom, in the end turn out to be *deterministic* because heavily influenced by external factors.

Someone will object that a tired man who gives up his rest to yield to his family's desire suffocates his own wish; thus he subordinates his action to the will of others and as a result is not at all free. [32]

In other words, it would seem from the example given that the individual is renouncing his own freedom, choosing an action he does not want to make, only to please his wife.

So then the question must be presented in other terms: was this choice *morally* compatible with this man? Was his conscience able to bear that decision to the point that, when all is said and done, it was a pleasure for him and not a sacrifice to decide at that moment to go out with his wife?

Already we can discern from these words that the same decision, ultimately, can be experienced in a different way by different people. Every person who experiences this scene, this situation, will react in a different way – choosing the first or the second decision – even while maintaining the same freedom of choice, because in essence for him there is no sacrifice or constriction. What changes is only the level of his conscience: in the last analysis, a more advanced conscience coincides with more advanced evolution.

In reality, given that the aim of existence, as we have seen, is the acquisition of a greater conscience drawn from the essence of the

---

[31] *Ibid.*, p. 93, paragraph 4.
[32] Florence Circle 77, *Le Grandi verità ricercate dall'uomo,* p. 38.

experiences assimilated, logic consequently leads us to suppose that a choice made in greater conscience, precisely because it saves us from future effects – in other words, karma – will give us greater freedom in the future.

The choice made altruistically (the second choice), instead of adding "sand" to the filter takes some away, so much so that for us this small suffering is nothing but a physical discomfort given by the tiredness felt in that moment, but that, with what *for us* is a small effort of will, we choose to compensate with the joy that comes from seeing our wife happy.

I emphasized "for us" to highlight the fact that another person could very well choose the first alternative not out of pure selfishness, but simply because this person has not undergone sufficient evolution to be able to bear what for him is too much effort, a suffering too much greater than the benefit of seeing his wife happy.

I add here that if his evolution were even less than this, the man would not only have chosen the first alternative without even thinking about it, but he would not even had had the *sensitivity* to appreciate his wife's happiness at going out, because this would not bring him any benefit, not even the pure altruistic joy in seeing her happy. He, quite simply, could not. It would not *actually* be one of his possible choices, since his conscience, highly deficient, would in that choice be totally overshadowed by his ego.

The noun *freedom*, semantically, means "the absence of necessity, coercion, or constraint in choice or action."[33]

It is beyond doubt that a person, seen "from inside," acts according to his will and without any constraints. However, he often is not aware of the subtle yoke of the influences and conditionings of the environment in which he lives. He does not realize that, probably, if he had been born in another place or another time or lived in another environment he would be not just a little but totally different in his thoughts and his choices.

Without dwelling too much on what will be treated in the chapter on karma, for now suffice it to say that the individual drives the dynamic of what he will go on to live as future experience, independently of the availability of real freedom of choice. *Indeed,*

---

[33] *Merriam Webster Dictionary*, Merriam Webster Inc., 2020.

the cosmic laws are broken whether the person acts of his own spontaneous will or whether he is influenced by something else.[34]

Put in other terms, it is not important *for the purposes of evolution* if a person is living a series of unexpected events by which he actually realizes his freedom is reduced to the point of being totally absent. Whether a person decides on the basis of an outside influence or ignorance or constraint, or even if he doesn't decide at all, submitting to a situation without any possibility of choice – the classic bolt out of the blue – for the purposes of evolution the experience will be acquired in any case.

"So then," one might ask instinctively, "what fault is it of mine if I make a mistake out of ignorance or constraint?" But life, we should keep reminding ourselves, is not a trial of the soul, but its growth. When all other signals have failed, the evolution of the conscience, as a learning method of last resort, does not aim at punishment but at painful direct experience.

The soul is not subjected to an experience, whether good or bad, to be tested on the basis of its reaction, but precisely the opposite is the case. Experience serves so that the person can draw from it what he can; repeated over time, these acquisitions will work so that the conscience no longer has to live similar experiences in the future, because of the evolution it has gained.

A certain degree of freedom, keep well in mind, exists and must always exist, but theoretically it has no influence for the purposes of evolution. Practically speaking, however, it does, because a person must always have, or at least must always believe he has in that moment, freedom in making his decisions, because this gives him a sense of responsibility towards his future.

In other words: seen from outside the physical plane, there are moments when a person enjoys true freedom and moments when his choice, albeit free and voluntary, is nonetheless influenced by external and internal conditionings – desires, preconceptions, emotions, the environment, etc. – to the point that he could not help choosing only that decision, a choice that was voluntary for him but really arose deterministically.

---

[34] Florence Circle 77, *Dai mondi invisibili*, p. 185.

To sum up: there are moments when a person is not free to choose, because events happen without a possibility of choice. In all the other moments, instead, an individual chooses freely.

However, the choices, even if free and voluntary, are conditioned by the environment, by what we have absorbed as our culture, by social preconceptions, by fatigue, by the emotion of the moment, by habits, our way of thinking, our character, and so on. All these conditionings, added together, make up, in the last analysis, our ego. Can a person escape his ego and choose to decide in a total absence of conditionings? In other words, can the conscience manifest itself as *pure* and without the influence of the ego? Clearly not. The ego is made up of the sum of the bodies: mental, astral, physical. The fact of having a physical body could influence us on the level of fatigue; having an astral body could influence us on the level of emotions and desires.

But note well: a person cannot escape his conditionings taken all together – they correspond to his ego – but can decide to escape a single conditioning. He can choose to escape the conditioning of the physical plane given by the tiredness of a full day's work, choose to make his wife happy by going out.

So we glimpse here the birth of a new definition of freedom: the freedom to choose not on the basis of something necessity, desire, or habit would like to make us choose, but to decide to restrain that conditioning – placing in full awareness a *de facto* limit on one's freedom of action – in order to act in accordance with his moral sense, with what his conscience is suggesting to him.

It is as though the individual forced his ego a little so as to follow his conscience a bit more; it is as though he voluntarily gave up a piece of his freedom, to donate it to the benefit of another creature.

Hence the decision to go out with his wife despite being physically tired.

This is perhaps the important point to understand: to be free it is necessary, first and foremost, to be free from ourselves; and to be free from ourselves and from external conditionings it is necessary, we have seen, that an individual manage to discover his truth, to know himself, to see himself as he acts and reacts, to understand his errors and make sure he does not commit them again, otherwise everything that has not been discovered will be carried with him wherever he goes, as a chain dragged around through the world.[35]

What does this mean? That the individual, when he makes the more altruistic choice, within the limits of his morality, is not depriving himself of any of his freedom, much less is he suffering because his choice involved a little bit of sacrifice. On the contrary, he will be happy about his choice because for him it is the right thing to do and because he will see, as in the preceding example, the happiness of someone he loves.

By choosing what is at bottom an altruistic act, giving up a small part of his ego, with that gesture he predisposed his conscience towards change; it is as though he had taken a few grains of sand out of the filter. But not only this: by that gesture, by that example, he also affected the sensibility of those around him; this means that he succeeded in predisposing others' conscience towards change. And all this with a simple choice that is a little more altruistic. Thus also his partner's conscience will be predisposed to change.

It should be made very clear: change is a slow and gradual process, and depends above all on the evolution of the individuals. Thus, it could happen that the tired fellow, by choosing to go out, manages to remove metaphorically ten grains of sand from his filter; while his wife, within the limits of her understanding and evolution, could very well remove twenty from hers, just as it could be that she only removes one.

What I want to say is that this gesture will have made a small inroad into her heart. And into her evolution.

There is another aspect to consider when we choose an altruistic gesture: Every time our conscience expands, it is as though our possibilities for future choices also increased, in that our sensibility and our moral sense, by growing, enable us to choose with a higher range of sensitivity, and in the future we shall be more predisposed to repeat the same altruistic choice whenever the opportunity arises.

That is to say, we shall have an easier time making a decision evading a similar conditioning because we shall be closer to understanding (metaphorically, there will be less sand in the filter).

A basic principle exists on which the evolutive mechanism of conscience is based: the degree of freedom a person has – the

---

[35] Ifior Circle, *Dall'Uno all'Uno*, vol. II, part II, p. 147.

concrete possibility of evading a necessity of the ego – grows in direct relation to his degree of sensitivity, in other words his level of conscience. In essence, freedom of choice grows in proportion to evolution.

From this derives the fact that not only will a more "aware" choice of action enable us to improve the quality of our life in the future but, thanks to that subtle but gradual broadening of the conscience that the experience just acquired will bring us, our "space" of freedom will increase.

Our actual freedom – understood as the possibility of choice – increases both *qualitatively* and *quantitatively*.

Thus the miserly individual, when he has overcome the feverish desire to possess more than others, will understand, at least in part, that his behavior did not consider others at all. He will understand this at his own expense, because the experiences, more or less painful, he has had will have been transformed into a higher, more "sensitized" conscience. So then, when other analogous experiences come up in the future, he will have a freer choice – in the sense of less conditioned. A filter that limited him will disappear, a veil will fall away, and he will look at others from different points of view.

It goes without saying that the increase in conscience brings with it an increase in knowledge, so that the person will have more tools suitable for reasoning in a more subtle and refined way when he comes up against a similar experience, whether his own or lived by others.

A more evolved individual means in essence an individual who embraces a higher morality. What correlation can there be between morality and freedom?

The moral growth of the individual makes him free not because it puts him in the condition to want or to do anything, but because it pushes him more and more towards what reveals itself to his conscience as an ideal of "good,"[36] that is to say the individual could make many more choices. Because his conscience manages to conceive, with his thought and reasoning, many more hypotheses, he sees many more paths to solve a given problem. He could, but his moral conscience would lead him to rule out immediately all the

---

[36] Florence Circle 77, *Dai mondi invisibili*, p. 184.

images, the solutions which might, for example, result in harm to another person.

This is what we were saying before about the man who was tired: he could very well stay home to rest, but his moral sense is such that he would suffer more than his physical tiredness, knowing that his wife had a desire to go out. By contrast, the joy he would get from seeing her happy would be greater than his tiredness.

With a little play on words, then, we could state that "the more evolved individual *could, but doesn't want to.* The lesser evolved person *would like to, but can't."*

This is logical; for if a lesser evolved person had great freedom, he would set in motion so many causes that they would suffocate him, while – since freedom is proportionate to evolution, which is to say to the conscience – a natural control exists which restricts the field of action of the unevolved so that they can only set in motion as many causes as would not suffocate them.[37]

But what would happen to the man who was tired in the event that he decided to stay home? We have drawn a picture of that man as if morally he had perforce to choose to go out with his wife, otherwise a curse would fall down on his head!

In reality, both choices are right in that moment for him – and by right I mean that they are calibrated to his level of evolution and to his morality – and both will result in the same evolution for this individual. But the first alternative (to stay home) would lead the individual to repeat the same experiences multiple times – and accumulate more "sand" – and in essence the same evolution would take a longer time to achieve and would entail a few more episodes of suffering. Conversely, repeating the altruistic choice would have as an evolutionary effect the shortening of time and a less "rocky" existence.

Both these choices are right for the individual because the choices are in any case conditioned by the ego present in that moment and thus by the level of conscience achieved. This is an important point to understand. Let's try to explain this with another example:

---

[37] *Ibid.*, p. 185.

1. A child is playing in the kitchen while his mother is cooking. At a certain point the child, moving his arm, accidentally knocks a glass to the ground and it breaks. His mother comes over to the child and, scolding him vigorously, sends him to his room as punishment. The child leaves his games and goes away, sad that he broke the glass and disappointed his mother.

2. The mother, going over to her child, understands that it was an accident and consoles the boy for having broken the glass. She explains to him that it wasn't his fault and that these things happen, and the next time both of them will be more careful to move things off the table before he starts playing. The child apologizes and smiling, wraps her in a warm hug.

What is happening? The story developed in two alternative ways, according to the mother's reaction. Let us hypothesize that the mother is an individual who has evolved to a greater or lesser degree for the purpose of evaluating reactions and consequences.

Is her first reaction a proper one? Without going into generic judgments about a policy of reproof and punishment, for a more evolved individual behavior like this is abominable: a mother like this is heartless. I agree; but a mother who has not evolved, with very little experience to support her conscience, in that moment will not conceive of anything other than an aggressive, punitive reaction. Because this is the way she was brought up, because this is the way you have to act to train your children, because this is the way she is by nature… and a thousand other reasons that she can find to justify her behavior. But then, is it right or not? For us no, for her absolutely yes. Morality is not the same for everybody, and it moves in tandem with a person's conscience. Thus, with her actions, she is in the right if she cannot manage to conceive of a higher kind. Will her act help her evolve? Certainly it will, certainly it will make her evolve, but by taking the longer and more painful path. It will make her evolve "by accumulation," because a moment will come in her life when, provoked over and over again by life in certain experiences, life will find no other remedy than a painful "correction" to remove the sand that has built up in the filter.

That is to say, she will experience, for example, the same pain that her child felt, inflicted on her by her boss, for instance, or her husband.

How many times has life proposed similar situations to the mother of the first scene, and every time, her choice fell on a crystallized freedom, without ever making an effort to find a better alternative? And yet that environment which has conditioned her so strongly to have that disposition has also tried many times to show her better ways of behaving, more ethical and more sensitive choices. So then, if we understand all this, we understand also that life at this point has no other remedy than to fall back on what will be an unpleasant experience for the woman, painful for her conscience, the only one capable of pushing her in the direction of greater understanding. These unpleasant experiences occur without her being able to avoid them; they are what we have called "absences of freedom."

The second reaction, it goes without saying, is the more evolved choice, the one a more sensitive, more conscientious mother would make, one who has already understood that certain coarse reactions are no longer suitable. This person, above and beyond the environment in which she lives, above and beyond the thoughts of other people, will always act in keeping with what her moral sense will indicate to her in her choices and her behavior, like the choice of the second alternative.

The causes set in motion will be more subtle in nature, and the evolution of her conscience will move in a much gentler way, without the need to live the unpleasant experience of the first alternative.

Before concluding the chapter, let us summarize:
- "So far as a man thinks, he is free," said Emerson. We can now state that man is free not only because he thinks, but because he *manifests* a conscience;
- to reach the point of manifesting a conscience, a person will have in the course of his lives many experiences that will make him grow spiritually; whatever choice he makes, he will evolve just the same;
- altruistic choices will enable him to shorten the time his evolution takes and to have "gentler" future experiences;

- the means available to a person to realize what are his "evolutionary filters" to be removed by making altruistic choices is "know thyself";
- a person's true freedom grows with the growth of evolution. The more the person manifests a higher conscience – which is acquired experience – the more this person can enjoy true freedom of choice, and the more opportunity he will have to escape the conditionings of his environment and his ego and the circumstances of the moment;
- an altruistic choice will enable not only the evolution of the person who makes it, but will help to favor the evolution also of the one who "receives" it;
- the more evolved individual does not want to do certain actions, because in him the sense of morality and responsibility towards others and towards himself has grown; he will seek out, among the various choices available to him, the one that is most altruistic and profitable for everybody.

Will

How does the question of will fit into all this discussion? What role does will play with regard to freedom?

Tradition says that the noted poet and writer Vittorio Alfieri had himself tied to his chair so that he would write his works; as a result he is even now held up as a clear, pure example of iron will, to the point that his line "volli, sempre volli, fortissimamente volli" (*I willed, and always willed, and strongly willed*)[38] is taught in schools and known to everybody who possesses a minimum of Italian literary culture.

Above and beyond whatever actual extension this anecdote might have, I hope that fans of Alfieri will not be angry with me if I, on the contrary, attempt the hypothesis that, all in all, someone who has himself tied to a chair to be faithful to a goal demonstrates, to my mind, many things but certainly not an iron will.

Would he maybe have preferred to chase some pretty girl, or play a game of dice in a tavern, or perhaps take a nice nap?[39]

It is certainly not the case with this distinguished writer, but perhaps a person who has himself forcefully immobilized so he cannot leave his desk for hours probably does this because he knows that his mind is subject to distraction and to invitations to do other, more pleasant things.

Semantically, having a will could be related to a "strong will to do something," but in reality will denotes a characteristic different from what common opinion holds it to be. *The individual who has a will is not the one who succeeds in doing what he wants, but one who, on the contrary, manages to do well what does not completely suit him.* Indeed, succeeding in doing what one wants, even only on a merely logical and rational level, does not entail, in reality, a

---

[38] This famous statement by Alfieri appears in his reply to Ranieri de' Casalbigi, written in 1783.
[39] Ifior Circle, *Sussurri nel vento*, pp. 43-44.

strong effort of will, but going against one's impulses, one's needs, one's egoism, to complete a predetermined task, undoubtedly conceals – on the part of the one who has to act – a significant amount of will.[40]

Thus a person who, for example, wants to become a doctor – because she feels a strong passion – but does not have an adequate cultural foundation, can become what she has always dreamed because she is driven by a strong force of will.

Will comes up wherever there is a contrast, a clash between differing factors. Does will reside in the ego? In light of what has been said, it would seem not to be; otherwise we could not explain all the cases in which, for example, a person risks his own life to save a person in danger. Will, at least what we are describing, resides in the conscience.

So it is that will, in the expression of its manifestation as *effective freedom*, is the possibility to remove oneself from a state of necessity and conditioning. *This is why will makes a person free.*[41] Will, in this sense, is the instrument of freedom.

Choosing to go out with his wife instead of staying home, making her happy even though he is tired, he makes an *effort of will*; he moves away from a physical need, moving his choice onto another, more *subtle* plane, the emotional and mental one. It is escaping a logical consequence of the physical plane, understanding that for us the satisfaction of a person who has been waiting for us all day is more important and that her disappointment would weigh on our mind more than our physical tiredness. It is only our achieved conscience that, activating more subtle planes than the physical one, makes an effort of will and evades a state of necessity.

---

[40] Ifior Circle, *La crisalide*, Genoa, Ins-Edit, 1991, pp. 217-218.
[41] Florence Circle 77, *Le Grandi verità ricercate dall'uomo*, p. 38.

Happiness

"A calm and humble life will bring more happiness than the pursuit of success and the constant restlessness that comes with it." This thought on happiness comes from Albert Einstein, and the paper on which he wrote it was sold at auction for a million and a half dollars.[42]

Even Einstein, who devoted his life to relativity in physics, realized that there is nothing more debatable than happiness, subject as it is to another type of relativity, that of feelings, human emotions, individual experiences.

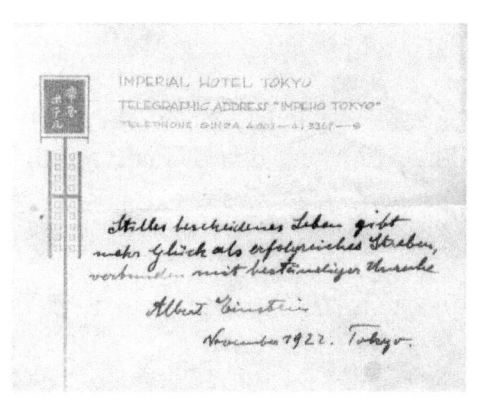

Fig. 2 – The sheet of paper on which Einstein wrote his notes (detail)

As commonly meant, the happiness to which one normally refers is principally the happiness of our ego, that is to say the feeling of gratification and the consequent state of transitory wellbeing when what we desire is achieved.

Helping to enhance this condition is also the physical manifestation of happiness, in which the sensation of satisfaction, fulfillment, wellbeing, is accompanied, from the strictly physiological standpoint, by an increase in certain hormones such as serotonin.

The fact that this state of wellbeing is not long-lasting – it seems

---

[42] Einstein wrote some notes on a sheet of stationery of the Imperial Hotel in Tokyo in 1922 as a gift to a bellhop in order to give him not an ordinary, vulgar tip in money but these handwritten notes in German, signed by the scientist himself. The sheet was sold at auction in Jerusalem on 24 October 2017, fetching the price of 1.56 million dollars.

47

strange to say – is a characteristic of evolution. The fulfilled ego places the astral body in a state of "excitement" and in turn, through the "interface" of the etheric body, various neurotransmitters are stimulated in the physical plane, including serotonin, which is why it is called "the happiness hormone." The temporary astral excitement dies down, serotonin diminishes with it, and the state of happiness is over. And so the individual – or at least his ego – moves off in a new pursuit of happiness, and the cycle starts over again.

It would be easy, children, to tell you that to be happy all you have to do is be content with what you have, but the answer cannot be so simple, in that it is part of the evolutionary necessity of an individual never to be content with what he has or, at least, to limit his contentment to brief periods, then to move on towards other new goals, other new objectives that make him think the satisfaction he has felt up to then is only a point of passage, by now no longer valid or fulfilling.[43]

If this continuing mechanism did not exist, the evolutionary process of every individual would be blocked, detrimentally, at the first satisfactions of the ego.

*"Between two viands, equally removed
And tempting, a free man would die of hunger
Ere either he could bring unto his teeth."*

says Dante (*Divine Comedy*, *Paradise* IV:1-3, translated by Henry Wadsworth Longfellow). If a man equipped with free will were not pushed into making his choices by a scale of personal satisfactions – such as happiness – which help him fulfill his ego on all three planes (physical, astral, and mental), he would not have anything spurring him to choose. Without the stimulus of conditioning – among all of them, happiness reigns supreme – a person would not be content to decide on one of the various alternatives offered him and would not choose at all.

Thus this continuous search for happiness leads an individual to ask himself questions, to move, to act, to interact with others and, as a result, to have experiences, one after the other, until he

---

[43] Ifior Circle, *Dall'Uno all'Uno,* vol. II, part I, p. 132.

accumulates the understanding useful for his evolution.

But there is another type of happiness which can be identified and has characteristics different from that of the ego, that is to say the happiness linked to the individual's conscience. This sensation of happiness is often perceived by the individual without his being able to identify where it comes from, and this is the consequence of the achievement of some understanding within his conscience. It is a sensation of inner peace very similar to that which saints have often called a "state of beatitude."

This happiness, the true happiness, comes from inside us; it is literally a state of being, and the only thing that can nourish it is the evolution of the conscience.

It is a happiness that never fades, that does not depend on any outside event or influence, acting as a background to the everyday life of a person who has achieved a certain degree of evolution.

Happiness, we can say, is the smile of the conscience that has understood.

From those notes, we can deduce that this was well understood also by Albert Einstein.

Karma

An ancient Buddhist maxim says: "If you want to understand the causes made in the past, look at the results as they are manifest in the present. And if you want to know what results will be manifest in the future, look at the causes that exist in the present."[44]

Karma. How trendy is this term in the West! And how much is it misused! Karma is used as a synonym of fate, punishment, trial; while in fact karma is only an "activity": it is nothing more nor less than an effect, a part of the chain of causes, so dear to determinists, which moves the life of beings.

Karma, then, is everything. It is not just an exceptional event that unexpectedly and involuntarily changes one's life. Karma is the glutton's stomachache, it is the muscle mass of a trained athlete, it is the blond color of a woman who has bleached her hair, it is the sprout from a seed planted in fertile soil, it is the burn felt when one gets too close to a flame, and so on.

Karma is not fate, if by this is meant something that happens without an explanation and without volition; it is not punishment, because in and of itself it is neither good nor bad. Karma is not a trial; if anything it is a teaching, because it completes the experience set in motion, and one learns from experience.[45]

Just as in physics there is the law that every action causes a reaction, karma is the analogous law of cause and effect in the spiritual realm: every action a person does provokes an effect that falls (positively or negatively) on the person who did it. The true target of karma is not the person as such, and it is not his physical action. Its aim is the person's conscience, because it is here that the experiences one has had on the physical plane have a bearing,

---

[44] From the sutra on the observation of the mind, translated between AD 785 and 810. In Indian literature, the sutras are treatises based on brief aphorisms, moral maxims, and philosophical elaborations.

[45] Florence Circle 77, *Le Grandi verità ricercate dall'uomo*, pp. 43-44.

reverberate, and are elaborated. The conscience, in keeping with any deficiencies or wealth it might have, is directed towards other experiences. Karma is only an exterior situation in the extent to which it serves to produce the inner ferment which brings understanding, and thus conscience.

Let's suppose that Tom is miserly. Firstly, he is this way because his conscience is not developed enough to keep him from being like this. Our miser will think like a miser, he will desire like a miser, that is to say he will feed a chain of causes in which every type of human activity is oriented towards miserliness: physical activity, sensation, thought. In what way will the repercussions of his activities affect him? Here, to answer this, we must know the reasons for his miserliness, above and beyond his lack of altruism. Suppose that it is not wanting to give to others, a desire to accumulate in order to be more than others. The causes set in motion will lead him, in effect, into situations from which he will understand that it is totally useless to have an unfettered desire for property and wealth; such an understanding will arise, for example, from living in a subsequent lifetime a situation in which he will experience the effects of the miserliness of someone in his circle and will be its victim. At that point he has learned not to be miserly, but he has not overcome the desire to stand out by seeming to be better than others. Consequently, he will have another lifetime in which, for example, he will think he can achieve the consideration and esteem of others by being extravagant [46] and wasteful. And so on. This is how karma acts, each time, as the effect of a cause he set in motion, but for the sole purpose of bringing him understanding.

It is mistakenly thought that karma is generated only when a wrong decision is made and that only then will it call down the painful effect. Such a view would be correct if pain were a punishment, but this is not the case: the only aim of karma is to push a person towards inner reflection.

And it is inner reflection, this process of "knowing oneself," that will slowly bring a person to make the choices, the "qualitative leaps" in the chain of cause and effect of which we were speaking earlier. Those qualitative leaps constitute an individual's true freedom.

Thus an individual who has already achieved a certain evolution

---

[46] *Ibid.*, p. 45.

makes qualitative leaps, that is to say because of his conscience he feels in such a way that enables him not to be inexorably dragged along by necessity, that enables him to live serenely what is for others a source of anguish. Nonetheless, this does not mean that the evolved person does not feel, for example, fatigue as an effect of a cause he has set in motion. However, he will experience that fatigue in a different way from a non-evolved person and will not be conditioned by it; he will know how to get rid of it in short order, but in any case he cannot avoid feeling it.[47]

Eastern peoples have known the law of karma for thousands of years. Nonetheless, some Eastern traditions have interpreted this law incorrectly and have come to the conclusion that one should never interfere with the karmic destiny of another person. This gross error of interpretation has permitted the spread of an indifferent mentality insensitive to the suffering of the weaker sectors of society when it was perfectly possible to do something to alleviate it. Moreover, the very refusal to lend aid in these circumstances produces karmic consequences for the person who refuses to offer help. In India, karma has been used to implement policies to manage certain situations of poverty in order to make the underprivileged castes live in full acceptance of their place in society. Thus someone in a precarious economic and social situation, by accepting in this lifetime the karma of "poverty," in a later life would be reborn into a higher, wealthier caste. Even if the concept of karma remains fundamentally true and real, the logic of this "karmic wheel" is altered by social and political aims, to the point that the karmic position is no longer clear of a person who, being reborn into a wealthy class, has no interest in listening to the cries for help from the poorer classes.

As for the West, *at the beginning of the Christian era, the first Fathers of the Church discussed at length the advisability of preaching to the members of the burgeoning Christian community the ancient truths concerning karma*[48] and reincarnation, a concept that is closely tied to it. After spirited debate, they decided to exclude these teachings from the doctrine because they realized the philosophical error made by some populations with an Eastern

---

[47] *Ibid.*, p. 47.
[48] Hilarion, *The Nature of Reality*, Crisalide, 1997, p. 54.

culture.[49] *This is the reason why Christian doctrine insists particularly on the commandment to serve one's neighbor in every way possible: by doing this, not only does one work off one's own karma, but it is possible to alleviate* (on a practical level) *the suffering of others.*[50]

Undoubtedly this decision was the right one for the times, taking into consideration the cultural and intellectual background of the people of that period and later. Even now, many people are satisfied with the definitions and justifications offered by today's Church, and it would not even be right to upset their minds with revelations that fall outside their tradition and that they would not be able to understand in the true fullness of their meaning.

But undeniably logic, together with a concept of justice and equity, imposes on an increasing mass of people the search for a more equitable truth than the one handed down to us by the Christian tradition.

Suffice it to think of the concept of Christ who, we are taught, was sent among men to take upon himself their sins and expiate these, freeing us from our sins.

It is my own personal idea that this is a somewhat fairy-tale view of life. Undoubtedly it is a beautiful and consoling image, one that above all gratifies the ego that holds it to be true because it makes that person feel protected, loved, important... and undoubtedly also relieved of responsibility.

But in light of what we are saying, this view seems hardly credible, besides being illogical: *if it were possible to take upon ourselves the guilt of another person and expiate it, we would certainly not work towards his benefit, given that this would not bring him any understanding of his errors but only a satisfying escape from his responsibilities, relegating to others the task of compensating for his faults.*[51]

Let's put aside for the moment this historical view of the topic and go back more specifically to examining the mechanisms of karma.

The individual who is subjected to karmic influence, especially

---

[49] As far as the Christian church is concerned, it was the Council of Constantinople in AD 533 that forbade any allusion to reincarnation and karma.
[50] Hilarion, *The Nature of Reality*, pp. 54-55.
[51] Ifior Circle, *Dall'Uno all'Uno,* vol. IV, p. 190.

when his conditioning torments his existence, tends always to reason as though the only karma that exists is negative and to forget that there is also positive karma, which is equally strong, equally important.

Besides, if it were true that the weightiest, most important, principal karma were only the negative one, in life we would never have even one sole instant of joy and happiness, serenity and tranquility. But luckily, every negative act we have done in some past lifetime and in the current one is matched always – sooner or later – by some positive, useful act, beneficial for others or our own family, which comes to re-establish a certain karmic balance, making our debits and credits begin to balance each other out and rendering our existence a swing back and forth between joy and sorrow, disappointments and moments of happiness.

We said earlier that *karma should thus not be considered a punitive (or rewarding) mechanism for an incarnate being, but a means to aid the individual's understanding about his behavioral mistakes, allowing him to experience personally the effects that this behavior has produced and, by experiencing them, draw from this a broadening of his way of feeling,*[52] his understanding, and as a result his evolution.

For karma befalls us to expand our conscience, to make us grow internally, to help us understand something that we stubbornly do not want to comprehend.

Observing karma from a different perspective from that of duality – negative karma and positive karma – we would have to admit that karma is always positive since it has the function of fostering the individual's understanding and consequently always of furthering his evolution.

The fundamental element for orienting karma towards our deficit of understanding is not action in and of itself as much as the intention that the individual has when he acts. It is intention that guides all of a person's activity, and it is this which has to be right and is therefore the object of the corrective effect of karma. Thus, the same action carried out by different people can give rise to different karmas.

If karma were limited only to the exterior manifestation of the

---

[52] *Ibid.*, p. 196.

individual, the effect would almost never hit the target because very often actions hide opposite intentions. Altruistic behavior that hides an egotistical purpose cannot bring about the same effect for both.

For example, much more praiseworthy would be the behavior of *an atheist who lives his life in the attempt to be fair and just without the incentive of a reward after death for his good behavior than that of a believer who acts justly and fairly not because he feels this is the best way to behave but because his faith will reward or punish him according to his actions.*[53]

Summarizing the working of karma, we can say that the elements which contribute to the formation of karma are:

- the individual's intention
- marginally, the choice of type of *action.*

Intention is the predominant element and the true target of karma. It is intention that manifests the individual's true desire. The same intention, the same inner motivation can manifest itself externally with actions very different from each other, simply because, above and beyond whether the intentions are altruistic or not, the action that results is in any case conditioned by the understanding achieved, by external influences, and by the level of culture reached. The element of intention is its foundation, but a certain value, even if marginal, is held also by the choice of the type of *action*. Let's look at an example: two mothers prepare a snack, spurred on by the same immense love for their child. One, moved by true altruistic intentions, prepares a fruit salad while the other gives the child a prepackaged snack cake containing preservatives and artificial coloring agents, which are not really good for him.

Their intention is the same, but the second mother will in some way have the duty and the opportunity, when her level of understanding permits it, to add to her knowledge of nutrition. In any case, her karma will be relatively light because her lack of knowledge was minor.

Karma would develop differently from this example in the hypothesis that this mother's intention were "polluted" not by ignorance but by a selfish desire to save time so she could spend it on her own pursuits, making her choose the shortest path: to keep

---

[53] *Ibid.*, p. 209.

buying packaged snack cakes. In this case, the karmic reaction will obviously be different and not so light.

Before, we started from the premise of identical intentions. In the opposite case, the very different intentions of the two women can result in an action that, seen from the outside, appears identical to an observer. This is the classic example of the altruistic gesture, the coin dropped in the offering plate in church that, while it indicates a praiseworthy altruistic act towards the needy, could hide the less praiseworthy intention of seeking approval and regard from others, even so far as seeking to put on a good show with the One who will have to admit them, so they hope, into Paradise.

Thus intention, in terms of the formation of karma, is much greater than the action manifested, which remains a marginal aspect. Action, to be carried out, has to be "coordinated" by the individual, passing through his cultural filters, beliefs, habits, and last but not least, undergo a certain "pollution" by the person's ego that perhaps may unconsciously hide ulterior aims. As in the hypothesis of the second mother, motivated by the same loving attention for her child but with a less advanced knowledge of nutrition than the first mother.

So then, from the interaction between intention and action different possibilities can take shape (see the table on the following page):

Intention:
1. The intention expressed by the individual is in harmony and balance between the person and others (altruistic intention, expressed conscientiously).
2. The intention expressed arises from the individual's ego, from some desire or need, and for him it is such a necessity that he cannot imagine otherwise (egotistical intention).

Action:
A. The action takes into account all the elements of the surrounding environment and is made in full awareness that what the person is doing is not harmful to him or others (more altruistic action).
B. The action takes into account mainly the ego's needs or is done out of ignorance or from a superficial analysis of the circumstances or by paying attention mainly to the person himself (more egotistical action).

		INTENTS	
		1) **Altruistic intent** (expressed through the conscience)	2) **Selfish intent** (expressed through the ego)
ACTIONS	**A) Altruistic act** (takes into account the environment and results in a benefit)	**1+A:** **positive karma** is created which leads to a positive "credit"; the conscience proceeds in evolution in harmony with itself and with the surrounding environment, without creating friction; the individual, within the limits of that sphere, expresses a high level of evolution and has understood properly	**2+A:** **negative karma** is created, but the conscience has useful information available for broadening its understanding because it can compare the positive effects of its action with the manifestation, not really altruistic, of the ego; The karma is **relatively slight** and easily resolved with more attentive self-analysis in the course of this same lifetime or the next
	B) Selfish act (takes into account mainly one's own ego)	**1+B:** **negative karma** is created **but it is slight**; it is a gentle karma that most times is understood and resolved in the course of the same lifetime, without great unresolved issues or suffering for the individual.	**2+B:** **Heavy negative karma** is created, which almost always will have an impact that is hard to resolve; It is a karma that generates suffering for the individual who experiences it, and generally several lifetimes are necessary before achieving a proper understanding and overcoming the lack that gave rise to this karma

Please note that this is an extreme schematization which, if on one hand it gives us a good idea of the formation of karma on the various levels, on the other *the reality is always much more complex, in that there is a wide range of possible variations.*[54]

Thus, broadly speaking, we can say that the individual can move by gradations from the case of 2+B in which a hypothesis of maximum suffering emerges, all the way to the case of 1+A in which there is a hypothesis of harmony and the absence of suffering.

Pain and suffering will be discussed in the next chapter.

---

[54] This schematization is taken from the Ifior Circle's book *Dall'Uno all'Uno*, vol. IV, pp. 213-214.

Pain

"Why did this happen to me? Why do I have to suffer?" In the moment when someone is suffering, there are no words to justify the misery and blockage that suffering brings. This is right and understandable. In the face of so much injustice, one remains as though paralyzed.

This is the ultimate weapon, we are told, *available to life to lead the individual to understand what he stubbornly refuses to understand.*[55] We are consoled by the fact that pain and suffering are never to be considered as punishments, but as a corrective push towards understanding. It is karma's last resort, the ultimate alternative that life holds in store for us, without which a person cannot overcome that aspect of life.

The best teacher within a person's lifetime is life itself: this is why we must reflect on our everyday life, on our surrounding environment, on our social relations with others.

To be sure, doing this entails very often finding ourselves face to face with ourselves, with our errors, our habits, desires, and needs. Sometimes it means admitting we have made a mistake, that we judged a person wrongly; it sometimes means having to give up or put off something we want, so that it would seem that a certain amount of suffering, sooner or later, becomes almost inevitable.

But life is a teacher, and the logic of life solicits the need for understanding, so that, if the final weapon of suffering were not activated, a person could spend their whole lifetime on Earth and not evolve even one step.

In the moment when pain comes, the person who is suffering cannot see reason. The believer loses his faith. The saint wavers. We are paralyzed, we curse and rebel. These reactions are fair ones, it is useless to say otherwise; indeed I would say that the opposite reaction is unnatural. But pain should not be endured passively. We

---

[55] Ifior Circle, *Dall'Uno all'Uno,* vol. I, p. 41.

are not our pain. We are much more than that. Pain should make us react; it should push a person to join with others who are close to him, it should spur him to work together with his neighbors to defeat other pain, his own and that of others.

The purpose of life is not pain; suffering is not some sort of trial, not punishment or divine castigation. Man, in portraying the divine, has always created God in his own likeness; the Most High is depicted with the same morality as the individual, since *men have believed that God, to impose His will, used the same method as that used by those in power.*[56]

Instead, it is necessary for people to understand that they have to work to seek more elevated moral means so as to have them available to deflect suffering away from themselves and all other individuals.

"Pain is given to you because God loves you," we are told. But this is faith that deflects from the true meaning of pain; it is a trap into which the ego falls.

Leading people to believe that pain is a test is much easier, in that this not only relieves the person of responsibility, but caresses and flatters his ego, almost as though he were a chosen one and this brings him closer to God.

"When does a person set in motion a painful karma? When, despite multiple warnings coming in from all sides, he does not understand and wants to experience directly. It is then that the painful effect becomes the only remedy for the individual to understand what his moral ideal is.[57] Thus he can add another piece to what his conscience has not understood; he can achieve an even higher moral ideal that will enable him, one day, to reach the point of understanding without suffering.

If a plant needed water, and watering it made it suffer, would it be merciful to let it wither and die so as not to make it suffer?[58]

The answer to this question gives us a glimpse of the solution to the problem of why human beings suffer.

Note well: suffering is not the only means to human evolution; many, many times a person is pushed by life towards an

---

[56] Florence Circle 77, *Oltre l'illusione*, p. 109.
[57] Florence Circle 77, *Dai mondi invisibili*, p. 166.
[58] Florence Circle 77, *Oltre l'illusione*, p. 113.

understanding and application of a moral ideal that enables him to live more and more in harmony. And if we look at the *individual economy*, it is right and desirable that *each person's interest be that of understanding without suffering, of using his mind without having to pay the price. This is not only possible, but represents what we must do.*[59]

What people have to do today is understand that, if the purpose of life is the evolution of their conscience, they must achieve this step by step, by learning first not to do to others what they would not like to have done to them, and then learning, as a higher moral step, that they must do to others what they would like to have done to them.

This does not mean that we must abandon everything we own in order to serve others, or any other extremism of that sort. *Understanding others means first and foremost understanding that no society can survive if each individual feels he is a sovereign despot at the center of the world.*[60] It is not necessary to stand out at all costs. What then should we do? Let us start small and close by, start from ourselves and those who are around us; let us start from the little things, the only ones for which we have no excuses.

It is not a simple act of giving that can light the way to evolution. A mere gesture will not make us better in our own eyes. *Giving away all that we own does not remove our desire to possess; renouncing honor and glory does not mean that we have overcome ambition.*

This is why it is important to know ourselves. If the person who gave up everything had analyzed his innermost being, had made himself aware that he was following his ego's ambition (to become great in heaven), that person would have spared himself and others disappointment and pain.[61]

Growing in conscience does not mean following useless religious rituals or imitating the deeds of who knows what spiritual Master. If a saint had the habit of reciting a particular prayer at a particular time of day, it is not by imitating him that we too shall reach enlightenment. Our religion gives too much importance to

---

[59] *Ibid.*, p. 93.
[60] *Ibid.*, p. 114.
[61] *Ibid.*, p. 125.

rite, but in the mechanical repetition of a gesture there is no inner reflection.

A very difficult subject to develop is the topic of suffering at others' hands. Let us start with an extreme case: if a person dies because of someone else's fault, should that someone else die too? Could he have avoided killing? How do you set all that in relation with their respective karmas?

First and foremost, the entire question starts from the basic premise that no creature can suffer at another's hands unless this was already karmically pre-established. This means that a person's freedom can *never* reach the point of establishing arbitrarily to take the life of another individual. The one who is a victim, because of his karma in that given moment, needed to abandon his physical body.

So then, how should we interpret a shootout, for example, from the viewpoint of the poor victims? For the karmic system, these people had terminated their physical cycle and had to move on. It is only an apparent coincidence that they found themselves in the place most likely to result in their death. This is the only valid alternative for understanding the teaching of karma. If the alternative, or someone's whim, were the case we would never even have got this far in our discussion.

The killer evidently did not have a sufficiently formed conscience to succeed in transcending his ego, his desire to obtain something from the victim or the situation. To his mind, killing was the best choice, the quickest one. And we have seen that the other creature had to abandon his physical body. But the fact that the victim "had to" die does not exempt the individual who kills him from being pointed to as a murderer.

It would be mistaken to believe that, since things were supposed to go this way and only this way, the one who kills bears no guilt. This does not exempt him from the responsibility that each person has towards his neighbor.

This is the way it had to be for the person who died, but not for the person who killed. For the creature who killed, not being able to overcome this action by means of reasoning, there was no other means than direct experience.[62]

---

[62] Florence Circle 77, *Dai mondi invisibili*, p. 191.

What will happen, on a karmic level, to the murderer? It is quite easy to understand that, in a future incarnation, he will have to die at the hand of another individual, closing his karmic cycle just as the creature who was killed closed his.

A person, in the course of his Earthly lifetime, wrapped up as he is in life and unexpected events, does not realize that he is accumulating many new experiences every day. When he passes on, he will understand the utility of his experiences; he will see again and understand the events of his most recent lifetime and will reconnect his karma to the events in his past lives that generated it. Only then, meditating on all that, will he become strengthened by the experience he has assimilated.

Reincarnation

This is the key concept of the evolution of the conscience. It would be absurd to expect a person to succeed in understanding and overcoming his own egotism in just one lifetime.

Reincarnation means that the individual, or better, his conscience, is born and reborn in various historical periods and different environments, with differing personalities and alternating between man and woman.

Reincarnation, in the west, was a widespread belief also in ancient times; suffice it to mention famous thinkers like Plato,[63] Pythagoras, Virgil, Cicero,[64] and so many other philosophers, historians, and scientists. At the time of Jesus, among the Jews the Essenes believed in reincarnation.

"Tell me, Lord, tell me, did my infancy succeed another age of mine that dies before it?... And what before that life again, O God of my joy, was I anywhere or in any body?" wrote Saint Augustine in his *Confessions*. And again, Origen of Alexandria, one of the acclaimed Fathers of the Church, described by Saint Gregory as "the Prince of Christian teaching in the third century," wrote: *"Every soul comes into this world fortified by the victories and weakened by the defeats of his earlier lives... His work in this world determines the place he will have in the next world."*

Reincarnation was accepted and taught until the Second Council of Constantinople in AD 553. On that date, by order of the emperor Justinian, who held himself to be the supreme head of the Eastern Church, Origen's doctrine was condemned and reincarnation was banned.

---

[63] The one who, more than any other, affirmed the cycle of earthly lives, necessary for achieving divine perfection, is Plato (427-347 BC). He states it in various of his works, especially *Phaedrus*, *Laws*, *Phaedo*, and *Meno*.

[64] Marcus Tullius Cicero (106-43 BC) writes about this in *De Amicitia*, *De Senectute*, and in a rare fragment of *Hortensius* which has come down to us.

Referring to the anathema of 553 against all those who believed in the pre-existence of the soul, Francesco Leti writes: "From that day the doctrine of rebirth was banned from the Catholic Creed and considered heretical. Nonetheless, despite invectives and excommunications, the doctrine was not totally uprooted from the West; the heretical sects that preserved the ancient tradition, and illustrious men, great philosophers, poets, scientists, openly agreed with it and defended it without pretense."[65]

From that moment on, the Catholic Church became the persecutor of the banned doctrines. Giordano Bruno, to cite one example, was burned at the stake because he supported two concepts considered heretical at the time: reincarnation and the plurality of inhabited worlds.

The reason for this exclusion on the part of the Catholic Church seems to lie not only in an ongoing process of simplification, as was already pointed out in the chapter on karma, but also for reasons connected with maintenance of the power of the Church over control of the absolution of the sins of the faithful and the sale of indulgences.

After this brief historical excursus, reality calls us back to our subject.

A doubt that arises, reflecting on reincarnation, is the reason for the necessity of being reincarnated in different historical periods and different places each time. First of all, it must be said that rebirths always take place along a forward temporal line, in other words it is not possible to skip from one era back to an earlier one. Reincarnation often happens in different places because the individuality, becoming incarnate on the physical plane, accomplishes its evolutionary journey by finding itself each time in the environment best suited to what it has to experience, the experiences it has to have in order to evolve.

The earliest incarnations always take place among peoples who are at a very low, primitive social and cultural level, because at the beginning of the evolutive process the things the individual has to understand are the simplest ones. Another thing it might be useful for us to know is the duration of the incarnations. Suffice it to think

---

[65] Quoted in Amadeus Voldben, *La Reincarnazione*, Rome, Mediterranee, 1999, p. 26.

that the individuality, from the savage to the enlightened one – from the first lifetime to the last – requires on an average about one hundred incarnations.[66]

The temporal interval, too, between one incarnation and another, changes significantly:

"In the beginning all the incarnations succeed each other quite quickly because in the beginning the individual needs to have the greatest possible number of experiences, and since these are all very simple experiences, easily assimilated, the interval between one lifetime and the next tends to be short. Bit by bit, as individuals progress in evolution and their evolution demands the comprehension of increasingly subtle concepts, they require a longer period of meditation on the part of the entity, after death."[67]

If we had to calculate an average, very roughly, of the time that passes between one incarnation and the next, the average would be about 350 years. Naturally, this is a number that should be taken only as a general indication; there can be incarnations in which the individual is born again soon afterwards, just as there can be those with an interval of 500 years or more.

For example, when the preceding lifetime was very short, in the next world the soul might have very little "material" to work through and assimilate, and in this case it is possible to be reincarnated without waiting a long period of time.

Let's suppose that a man was incarnated in the nineteenth century and had two sons who, even though destined for an early end, out of neglect, lack of attention or in any case a lack of altruistic love, died at a tender age. It is evident that this man would have generated a heavily negative karma for himself which he would have to work off, let's suppose, in the next life. This individual, when reborn, would have a very short lifetime, passing on right in the moment of happiness when he feels a strong attachment to this life. After his passing he will be able to meditate on what has happened, compare his happiness with the happiness his children missed, and from this understanding and assimilation make up for what he was not able to give in his preceding lifetime.

All this takes place within the framework and with the aim of

---

[66] See Ifior Circle, *Dall'Uno all'Uno,* vol. II part II, p. 224.
[67] *Ibid.,* p. 225.

teaching, never of punishment.

Another aspect to clarify in reincarnations is that when we are reborn we do not inherit in any way any character trait or physical characteristic that we had earlier. This would not make any sense due to the fact that each incarnation, since it always has to guarantee new evolutionary experiences, needs each time to recreate *ex novo* the mental body, the astral body, and consequently the physical body of the individual. What remains unchanged is only the conscience. In the event that one wanted to recognize something in someone's personality, more than in their character, we would have to look at the tendencies, interests developed, type of studies chosen, and possible talents manifested already in childhood.

Only occasionally can we find in the new body some small somatic characteristics similar to certain events or situations in the preceding lifetime, but this happens simply as a result of an effect of the law of karma.

When we talk about past lives, generally the first curiosity that comes up is if there is any possibility of knowing who we were in earlier incarnations. Without doubt, seeking to know oneself is what each person must do, but this search is not facilitated at all by knowing who we were. Precisely because of the fact that evolution always proceeds in a forward direction with each incarnation, it is not constructive to know how egotistical and how much worse we were in the past. What use would it be to know we were a friar, when maybe we did it without a vocation but only to escape a certain situation? Or to know that we were a valorous medieval warrior when the most that we could conceive then was a life of war, violence, and atrocities?

Only when you have understood the present will you be able to intuit the past and glimpse the future. Only when you have become aware of your current egotism will you understand how egotistical you were in times past and how much less egotistical you will be in the future.[68]

Nor should we be ashamed of what we were, in the sense of feeling guilt for having been overbearing, violent, and egotistical in past lives. Rather, we should thank the law of evolution, according to which we can now understand that those things were cruel and

---

[68] Florence Circle 77, *Per un mondo migliore*, p. 54

should not be done.

It could happen, at times, that we have reminiscences, instants of *déjà-vu*, flashes, sensations, or attitudes that re-emerge into our present day. In those moments the conscience is granted, so to speak, the possibility to remember something, perhaps stimulated by the surrounding environment, which stimulates the surfacing of something from earlier lives. *This happens precisely to spur that person to reflect, to meditate on his life and to understand that it is not true that we only live once.*[69]

So, for example, if it happens that we have a special liking for certain historical periods, certain foreign languages, certain places in particular, it could mean that in that period or those places we had earlier lives that were very happy and comfortable; it is almost as though we felt nostalgia for them. In the opposite sense, sensations of unease or dislike for certain places or times could hide incarnations in hard lives or tumultuous periods. Reminiscence is without doubt more frequent, in general, when it concerns a life that was a happy one.

Why is there this swing back and forth between happy and difficult lives? In the evolutionary cycle of each individual *there are always lives of action and lives of reaction.*[70] There is always this alternation in reincarnations: a happy life full of satisfied desires is followed by an unhappy life, often marked by suffering. There are active lives in which one "collects," so to speak, and passive lives in which one "pays." This is true especially at the beginning of evolution and up to a certain point of the evolutionary cycle; up to that point the individual will tend, in the active lives, to "accumulate" negative karma that will then have to be "paid for" in the following life, which perforce will be passive and filled with suffering. As evolution advances, the conscience, by growing and understanding, will no longer feel certain preponderant egotistical desires; its thoughts will be more refined and balanced, and the individual will no longer set in motion so many heavy causes that will need to be understood, at his expense, in subsequent incarnations. Thus, advancing even more in evolution, within the scope of one lifetime there may be active periods and negative

---

[69] Florence Circle 77, *Maestro, perché?*, p. 64.
[70] *Ibid.*, p. 65.

periods, since karma, having grown lighter, can be well understood in the course of one single life.

So this explains why there seem to exist cases in which life does not offer anything good, "unlucky" lives, and very happy lives, blessed by fortune; or even there may seem to exist people who do not undergo the consequences of their bad actions. All this is due to the individual's evolutive needs. But we can be sure that the moment of understanding comes for everybody, and then the situation will be reversed and the individual will have a lifetime of expiation.

Keeping in mind this necessity of evolution, it will be easier to understand the karma of creatures and to see that this karma truly exists. And knowing that the karmic law of cause and effect exists has the sole purpose of making clear to the individual the order that reigns in the cosmos, God's justice. Only this purpose, and no other.[71]

If a person is satisfied with believing that we are born in order to be set in front of good and evil and on the basis of our choices we earn eternal bliss or hell, if a person believes this, then in essence he has no need to believe in reincarnation – it is only a useless complication for his way of living and thinking.

If, instead, we hold that life is a continuous evolution, then we understand that one sole lifetime is not sufficient: it is necessary for us to have many experiences and the time to assimilate them, for us to understand our errors, to have many different points of view available to us for working through and overcoming our egoism and our personal profit, to understand that our neighbor should be treated like ourselves, that in life we are called to do our duty, and that we should approach others not because an external morality or a religion tells us we have to act in this way, but because we are spurred in our innermost being by a sense of love and altruism.

If a person feels in his heart that this is the right path, he understands also that in the plurality of existences lies also the justification that alone explains all the apparent injustices which otherwise, in the span of just one lifetime, would be unexplainable.

---

[71] *Ibid.*, p. 66.

Passing on

The time has now come to approach the topic of passing on, considered as the abandonment of the physical body and the subsequent life in the afterworld. Let's see what happens to the individual between one reincarnation and the next.

What happens to the conscience at the moment of passing on? Briefly, the experiences one has on the point of death have been amply documented in the book by the physician and psychologist Raymond A. Moody, *Life After Life*.[72] It contains anecdotal accounts of 150 people who came back to life after being declared clinically "dead."

Invariably, upon awakening these people recounted stories that were more or less identical, characterized in the vast majority by the following phases:

- viewing their body from above;
- observing objects and persons in the hospital room and the rooms nearby; listening to what the persons present were saying;
- a sense of extreme lightness and wellbeing and the perception of living out of their body (OBE: Out of Body Experience);
- going through a mainly dark tunnel at the end of which was a lighted opening;
- seeing at the exit of the tunnel a being of intense light and peace who reveals that this is a Guide;
- a vision of the afterworld, described as a world of intense light or a landscape of grassy meadows;
- seeing their deceased relatives approaching them;
- the forced summons back to life and the resulting

---

[72] See Raymond Moody, *Life After Life*, San Francisco, HarperSanFrancisco, 2001.

displeasure at having left this place and sense of wellbeing;
- upon their return to life, the ability to describe the movements and words of the doctors and others present in the hospital room and those nearby, which coincides with reports by witnesses.

These accounts, all of them very interesting, still present a "structural" limit in the fact that the experiences, being limited to the return to life, cannot report a fully exhaustive description of the afterworld. First of all, we cannot speak of a true death, since the connection with the physical body is not severed. Even if the astral body goes away temporarily, the etheric body is still present and connected, acting as an interface between the physical and astral bodies. Furthermore, if the individual comes back to life, evidently *he was not supposed to die: no matter how badly the body functions, has grave physical deficiencies, and is at the end of its strength, no one can die before or after the precise moment in which this has to happen.*[73]

This does not lessen his experience, in that the individual lives his Near Death Experience (NDE) as though he had really died, and this is confirmed also by the fact that the experiences lived are effectively the same as those of a real dead person. In fact, very often the individual comes back from the near death experience "changed".

This discussion, it should be clear, does not have the ambition of convincing those who do not believe in a life beyond death. No discussion can give certainty to someone who does not feel it to be true in his heart, and this is entirely right and proper. *There cannot exist proof that does not leave open, in some way, the path of doubt in someone who does not already believe firmly.*[74]

Physical death is not like a switch that you turn off, but is more similar to taking off your clothes: nothing of the true essence of the individual is lost except the physical clothing.

Schematically, death entails the following events, in succession, each with its own modes and time frame that we shall go on to analyze:

---

[73] Ifior Circle, *Morire e vivere*, Genoa, Ins-Edit, 1992, p. 44.
[74] *Ibid.*, p. 17.

- separation of the soul (the astral body) from the physical body and the resulting transfer of the conscience into the astral body;
- the experience of seeing, from outside, the body which has just been abandoned;
- the sensation (frequent but not present in every case) of passing through a "tunnel";
- a vision of pleasant landscapes and a subsequent phase in which every desire is experienced and fulfilled;
- a phase of "interrogation" *to which the individual is invariably subjected halfway along his journey of ascent. It is difficult to translate into human terms the questions that are asked, but they could be summarized as follows: "What have you learned in this life, and whom have you helped?"*[75];
- the meeting with deceased loved ones and other entities who will have function as Guides in the higher planes.

In this chapter we explore in detail the phases of passing on. In the next one we shall look more closely at the details of life in the afterworld.

When we die, we simply set aside our physical body, and with the exhalation of our last breath the soul (that is to say, the astral body) quickly leaves the body, taking the conscience with it.

All over the physical body of each individual are thousands and thousands of tiny points, which are set up to receive and transmit the vibrations between the physical plane and the astral plane.[76]

These tiny points are called *"nadis"* and are located in the *etheric body.*[77] At the moment of death these tiny points, which emit *electromagnetic vibrations,*[78] gradually stop functioning, as though switched off *electrically*; the astral body (the soul) gradually finds itself disconnected from the physical body. This is why the individual, after passing on, still feels tied to his physical body for a

---

[75] Hilarion, *Seasons of the Spirit*, Spigno Saturnia (LT), Crisalide, 1992, pp. 103-104.
[76] Ifior Circle, *Morire e vivere*, p. 72 par. 1.
[77] The etheric body is the seat of bio-vital energy and is responsible for the individual's state of health. An illness can present itself many weeks earlier in the etheric body as an energy imbalance.
[78] Ifior Circle, *Morire e vivere*, p. 72 par. 2.

certain period of time – on an average 36 hours – after his death. This is the time necessary for the *nadis* to be turned off. After this period the etheric body – which as we shall see[79] is still material, but at a much more subtle level of vibration – melts into the physical plane and the soul is completely uncoupled from the material world.

As confirmation of this, recently various scientists have recognized that electromagnetic activity (and not only in the brain) continues even many hours after clinical death, as reported in a study published by several researchers in Canada in issue no. 44/2017 of the *Canadian Journal of Neurological Sciences*.[80] This happens precisely because these tiny bio-electromagnetic centers of the etheric body – the *nadis* – are shutting down.

While the etheric body is progressively being extinguished, the individual's conscience has already at the moment of death moved into the astral body. After death, without any interruption in our sense of being, we leave behind only our material shell and find ourselves in a much lighter body, without the pains and toils of the physical body, but with an identical aspect to the physical cloak we had worn – so identical that often the person who has just passed on does not even realize it and does not believe that he is "dead." For that matter, the sensation of being alive is so strong, just as it was earlier with the old physical vehicle, that he tries to make people notice him and makes efforts to attract the attention of the people around him – people close to his body – who clearly cannot hear anything and can only continue to see just the physical body. *Finally the person gives up trying and accepts that there is evidently something "different" about his state, even though he feels exactly like the same person he was before.*[81]

Many will see similarities with the opening scenes of the 1990

---

[79] The etheric body, as we shall have a chance to portray in the second part of the book, is closely tied to the physical body and has a direct influence on it in that it is still a substance in the physical plane, but in a much more rarefied state.

[80] L. Norton, R.M. Gibson, T. Gofton, C. Benson, S. Dhanani, S.D. Shemie, L. Hornby, R. Ward, G.B. Young G.B., University of Western Ontario, Canada, *Electroencephalographic recordings during withdrawal of life-sustaining therapy until 30 minutes after declaration of death* (https://www.ncbi.nlm.nih.gov/pubmed/28231862).

[81] Hilarion, *Threshold*, Spigno Saturnia (LT), Crisalide, 1992, p. 52.

movie *Ghost*.

If a person cannot manage to move past the phase of acceptance of his new condition (many do so immediately) because of, for example, a particular attachment to the material aspects, habits, or beliefs of when he was alive, then at this point the "helpers" intervene; these are entities designated for this purpose, or more often relatives and friends who have passed on before him and can help him to overcome this moment and gradually become fully aware of his new situation.

Once this period is over, the ties with the physical world bit by bit (or rapidly) are loosened and the moment comes to realize the existence of a new dimension, the one immediately after the physical plane: the astral plane (or the plane of the soul). Put simply, the individual's conscience, which before the abandonment of the body was stationed in the physical plane, now moves into the astral plane. Thus it is not the astral body that travels from the material to the astral plane. Nor could it be otherwise, since every body remains within its own plane because it is made up of that type of matter. So it is only the conscience that "changes home."

The individual will then feel something like a sense of suction, drawn towards what seems to be a dark tunnel (however, not everyone has this experience). This corresponds with the conscience's passage through the dense layers that surround the Earthly plane. An intense white light marks the end of the tunnel and arrival in the astral plane.

In this phase, he will pause for a while – a period of time that is undetermined and varies from individual to individual – because he will have to face the sudden tide of all his sensations, all his desires, all his passions; besides, when he realizes that these desires and passions can give him temporarily everything he desired and all the sensations that he had always tried to have, he will build himself a world – his own personal one – made up of his own personal passions, to which he will attach himself.[82]

Opening before his eyes will be a world not too different from the physical world, but that has one different characteristic: the essence of the astral plane has the peculiarity of taking shape under the impulse of the emotions, sensations, and desires of each person.

---

[82] Ifior Circle, *Morire e vivere*, p. 38.

Thus each person builds for himself a world of his own, apparently solid, colorful, with smells, temperatures, sounds.[83]

Thus, a Christian will dream of the paradise promised by his religion, a Native American will see green pastures, a Buddhist Nirvana, and so on.[84]

This new place, where for the most part a state of happiness prevails, is set up to *encourage the abandonment of the old masks and inhibitions, facing and dissolving the unharmonious emotions and thoughts generated during life on Earth.*[85] For example, if a woman during her life had always desired to become a famous writer, in the astral world she will be given the possibility to fulfill her dream. She will build, with her strong desire, a world in which she will live life as a writer, the happy moments when she receives the recognition she sought, the acclamation of fans, autographs: everything that the woman's wish can express will come true.

The purpose of this concession does not lie in the desire as an end in itself to make the woman happy by becoming a writer, but to enable her to get rid of this intense desire which could be an obstacle impeding the further progress of her soul.

Here we should open a brief parenthesis: even if the desire, after having being lived thoroughly on the astral level, is greatly attenuated, this does not mean that the conscience has *overcome* that aspect. In other words, the deficiency of conscience which generated that desire in the last lifetime dissipates only when all the experiences and counter-experiences have been had – on the physical level – and, analyzing them, the individual has not only understood, but above all assimilated and thus moved beyond that aspect.

A person who was a glutton during his life, as a reaction will have in his new incarnation a new personality that maybe will lead him to be extreme in certain decisions and choices regarding food, precisely in order to experience the opposite; after death he will proceed once again duly to make his reflections and assimilations in the afterworld. Only then, in his subsequent life, will he be born again with the proper balance in the realm of food and nutrition. The

---

[83] Florence Circle 77, *Dai mondi invisibili*, p. 175.
[84] *Ibid.*, p. 174.
[85] Hilarion, *Threshold*, pp. 52-53.

vain person who in the preceding life was able to experience his vanity with an attractive body – in that he had the possibility of having an "active" life[86] – in his new incarnation will have to deal with a new physical appearance, a new environment; and in the comparison with the positive and painful experiences of the two lives, he will have the opportunity to overcome or at least attenuate the deficit of conscience that caused his strong desire for vanity.

Experiencing astrally the desire for the purpose of attenuating it is, meanwhile, necessary and functional only for the continuation of the conscience in the astral plane, since an excessively heightened desire would not allow a real life in the astral plane. In fact, the matter of the astral plane changes easily under the impulse of desire. Imagine for a moment all the inhabitants of the afterworld intent on experiencing their desires all together: some build castles, some create environments dreamed up by their ambition, some wrap themselves in situations they desired... Each one closed up in himself, living what he believes to be the real world, and in the end they really never encounter one another. It is clear that they will not have any way of meeting each other in one sole, shared environment until the desire of each one has been attenuated.

Let's go back again to the example of the woman who wanted to become a famous writer. After a certain period of time this woman will begin to feel satiated with this experience; she will begin slowly to realize that, if on one hand that life is too perfect to be real – as though something were missing – on the other the total fulfillment of her desire will begin to make her lose interest, and her desire will dissipate towards other involvements. And it is this way for all the other desires; little by little the individual will strip away, as though they were clothes, his denser astral wrappings that had formed in his life with his most intense and strong desires.

Thus, someone who in life loved to eat and drink in an exaggerated way, in the astral world will find his "paradise." His will, together with his strong desire, will be enough to make the food he has always wanted and all the wine he could wish

---

[86] The Guides have lovingly repeated to us that existences can alternate between "active" lives and "passive" lives, happy lives in which the ego's unbridled desire risks making us pile up negative karma, and tormented lives which come to collect on the karmic debt.

materialize, and for as long as he wants them, days and weeks, until it seems he will never be satiated. Here too the individual little by little, as his fulfilled desire starts to diminish, will realize that something is not right; the situation will begin to seem absurd to him and he will begin consciously to free himself *on an emotional level* of everything that tied him to the material plane during his life.

In the astral plane we find ambitions in all the social categories: creatures who were priests of some religion not because of a vocation but moved by ambition; here, in the astral plane, they create for themselves churches and monasteries of which they imagine themselves to be the rectors: politicians who imagine themselves heads of government, vain people who create for themselves a court of admirers of their beauty, and so on.[87]

Clearly these are "easy" examples. Reality is often made up of more complex habits, harder to overcome since the ego tends always to hide and justify itself. Thus, *a desire that remains long unsatisfied can require many years (measured in terms of linear Earthly time) of satisfaction on the astral plane before it is completely exhausted.*[88]

When an individual has finished experiencing all his unsatisfied desires, all his fantasies and unfulfilled aspirations – and has consequently stripped himself of his denser astral vehicles – he will finally be ready to meet the Guide who has aided him on a spiritual level during his lifetime (his Spirit Guide, or what the Christian religion calls a "Guardian Angel") and the other spiritual assistants who will help him in the subsequent phase of re-examination of his life.

In this phase it is as though the individual has recovered his memory after amnesia and remembers all the salient phases of his preceding life (and any other lifetime connected by karma to the last one), relived in minute detail. The individual thus sees again, as in a movie, the most important episodes of his last life, for the purpose of realizing the moral errors he made, but also his good deeds. From this examination, the individual will draw a *self-judgment* about his behavior. The one who judges will be the individual himself, not the Guides; no one but he, in accordance with the measure of his

---

[87] Florence Circle 77, *Dai mondi invisibili*, p. 176.
[88] Hilarion, *Seasons of the Spirit*, p. 110.

morality and not that of others, will judge his past life. The judgment will be very important for the period to come and for his subsequent future incarnation, so much so that it can cause him displeasure and strong emotion when he has realized instances of the wrong behavior in situations or towards persons which he could not comprehend when he was alive and that now, reviewed from different points of view and compared with the karmas set in motion, he now succeeds in understanding.

It has to be said, though, that the individual who finds himself judging his life will not relive all the scenes of his latest existence, but *unconsciously effects a sort of selection among the actions he has done, choosing those that in reality he can manage to understand.*

To be sure, the actions he did in life will be reflected later in subsequent lives as karma, however he will not be aware of these until the reaction that he set in motion presents itself to him at a time when he is capable of understanding it.[89]

At this point an explanation is necessary. First of all, we have said that it is not that an individual, having left the physical plane and reached the afterworld, suddenly has everything clear in his mind and instantaneously acquires new truths. So then, if the individual remains essentially what he was in the act of judging himself, *what sense does it make to review one's life? It would be as though a person, in old age, looked back: to be sure, while a certain percentage can recognize where they went wrong, 99% will try to justify themselves. And this is sometimes because they are not honest with themselves and always try to find an excuse, but other times precisely because they do not realize the suffering they unwittingly inflict on others.*[90]

This is why the individual, to be helped to realize where he erred, not only is immersed into the scenes of the earlier life, but is allowed to see them and "relive them" contemporaneously, as in a 360° vision, from his own point of view and that of the person who was the object of his error, making him feel the same emotional consequences and pain of that other person. Only with this will the individual realize his error, and he will be very sorry, but his

---

[89] Ifior Circle, *Morire e vivere*, p. 58.
[90] Florence Circle 77, *Maestro, perché?*, p. 30.

conscience will not yet be perfected in that aspect. In fact, it is only by personally reliving the event in a future physical life that he will be able, after the necessary rehashing after his death, finally to transcend the deficiency of conscience that led him to make a mistake. Only then will the individual never make the same mistake again in future lives.

To explain, I cite as an example an episode taken from the book *Morire e vivere* (*Dying and Living*) by the Ifior Circle of Genoa. A person who had passed on was stuck in his self-judgment, examining and re-examining, over and over again, an episode that had struck him particularly: the theft of a roll from a bakery. It is not that the theft of a roll in and of itself is such a serious act compared with other episodes in his life, but this entity, still fairly unevolved, had been upset by it; *he had committed that act not out of hunger or need, but simply out of spite or the impulse to do something bad, and this, at his level of evolution, presented truly a big obstacle, a big block, a big knot to be unraveled.*[91]

So this petty theft enabled him to carry out a self-analysis, offering him the understanding of an aspect of himself that he had not yet understood and that will help him make the little qualitative leap in the evolution of his conscience that will enable him to deal with aspects that are for him more complex in his subsequent lives. Then this entity, still a beginner, having finished his re-examination of this and other aspects of the life he has just lived, will understand, always within the limits of his comprehension, the causes set in motion in his preceding lives, comparing them with the effects experienced in his latest lifetime; he will view them also from the standpoint of the suffering inflicted on others and from this he will be able to draw his conclusions and learn his lesson. When the individual has been stripped of his densest astral vehicles – his strongest desires – he will be able to approach finally the true life of the astral world. Here he will encounter his loved ones who passed on before him and all the inhabitants of the astral plane; here he will recognize also the persons with whom he had a karmic or emotional bond in his earlier lives. He will be able to see, if he so desires, what happens in the physical world. His wish to see a loved one who is still alive will be sufficient to open up a window, so to speak, onto

---

[91] Ifior Circle, *Morire e vivere*, p. 59.

Earth. Clearly this contact will be unilateral and the loved one will not be aware of his presence, unless that person has a particular sensitivity, something that is still quite rare at our planet's current stage of evolution. When he has stripped away even the last layers of astral material, the individual will have slowly overcome also the most strictly emotional part of his life. At this point his permanence in the astral plane ends and he will wish to continue his existence further beyond. He will find himself then on the threshold of the mental plane.

"Once you get to the mental plane what happens?" What happens is that one will no longer have, practically speaking, the direct, immediate, and overwhelming effect of sensations and emotions, but his thinking will be more lucid, reflective, rational, and free from the other possible tethers; here, as he had done in the astral plane, he will re-examine his life once again, this time stripping away from it all the emotional part and seeing it rationally and clearly.[92] On a rational level he will be able to hide from himself absolutely nothing of what led him to act during his life.[93]

In this plane, too, he will be able to live situations that are enjoyable for him, but they will all be situations only of a mental type, since we remember that the part pertaining to emotion and the expression of desire has by now been left behind in the astral plane. *Scholars have their paradise in the mental plane: here the individual can pursue learning and satisfy his thirst for knowledge more than was possible as an incarnate being; in essence, he completes the notions he had in his latest incarnation.[94]*

"And of all that the individual learns in the mental plane, what remains?" The fruits of his reflections on the meaning of his life remain; whatever the individual was able to learn and know in the mental plane remains in the form of the impulse or facility to learn in a future incarnation. It will never happen, however, that an individual can evolve spiritually and begin something new in the mental plane, or in any case after his passing, because if this were the case, life on the physical plane would no longer have meaning.[95]

---

[92] *Ibid.*, p. 38.
[93] *Ibid.*, p. 73.
[94] Florence Circle 77, *Dai mondi invisibili*, p. 178.
[95] Florence Circle 77, *Le Grandi verità ricercate dall'uomo*, p. 177.

Moreover, the individual who lives consciously in the mental plane, besides seeing the other inhabitants of the mental plane, always has the possibility of seeing what happens in the astral plane and what happens in the physical plane. Every plane always has the possibility to see, besides that plane itself, all the planes beneath it.

Little by little the individual overcomes this phase too, and moving beyond it he will strip away also his mental matter, until he reaches the plane of the conscience (also called the *akashic plane*).[96]

Leaving behind the mental plane, the individual will have left behind all that made up the ego of the preceding incarnation. Reaching this point, the individual identifies himself solely with his conscience.

The akashic plane is the plane where all the experience which the individual has accumulated in his past lives resides. In synthesis, the akashic plane is the individuality's conscience, the essence of his evolution. Here vibrates only the matter of the conscience.

Now, if the entity has a low degree of evolution, this also means that he does not have a developed conscience and thus cannot live this plane in a conscious manner and will fall into a particular state, a sort of sleep that can last even a long time, until he finds that he has been incarnated again.

The reason why this individuality cannot live this dimension consciously lies in the fact that, at a low degree of evolution, the personality of the individual when he is incarnate will be shaped in large part by his self-centered ego and very little by his conscience. Here the example of a container comes to our aid.[97]

We know that the ego is shaped by the sum of the physical, astral, and mental bodies. They are created specifically at every incarnation for the purpose of creating the ego, the character and the physical form that will permit, through karma, certain experiences that will then be assimilated by the conscience for the purpose of making it grow. The individual with a low degree of evolution evidently, having reached the akashic plane, will not have put together enough "matter" of the conscience to be awake since *we have said that the ego is made up of the physical, astral, and mental vehicles that the individuality will no longer possess when it reaches*

---

[96] Akasha is a Sanskrit term which means "the basic essence of all things."
[97] See the chapter on human freedom.

this point.[98] We must always keep in mind that when we speak of the physical, astral, and mental planes we are always talking about the *transitory ego* and not about the individual's true being, whose essence is given by the sum of his experiences that have made up, over time, the akashic body, the individual's true core.

If the entity has a sufficient level of evolution (as is the case for a good many of the people incarnate on this planet), he will actively live the plane of the conscience; he will be able to encounter the other individualities that inhabit the akashic plane, acquaintances and family members from his latest lifetime but also those who were his relatives and friends in all his preceding incarnations. Here the entity can review his past incarnations, compare them, and discover the motives that determined the various karmas and that connect the causes set in motion in one life and the effects experienced in another. At this point, after a time that is more or less variable according to the need for an evolutionary interval, the entity will begin to feel something like a call to new material experiences which will predispose him towards a return to the physical plane by means of a new incarnation. A new mental, astral, and physical body will be recreated, and the person will have available new *vehicles for learning* in order to have different experiences that will further enrich his conscience from new perspectives. A new cycle begins again.

---

[98] Ifior Circle, *Morire e vivere*, p. 39 note 2.

Life in the afterworld

Now that we have examined the phases of passing on, let's see in detail what the afterworld is like and how the disincarnate live.

First of all, it must be reiterated that the individual, once he has left his physical body behind and arrived in the afterworld, does not suddenly become better and kinder or embrace greater truths than when he was on Earth. In the afterworld, the individual remains exactly what he was in the Earthly plane, since he carries with him all the ideas, habits, preconceptions, prejudices, desires, thoughts, and knowledge that he had when he was incarnate. This is because the individual loses only his physical body, but the astral body (where desires and emotions reside and which governs them) and the mental body (the seat of thoughts and reasoning) still remain present. The person remains the same as he was on Earth. Here he can meditate and reflect, still have a life of sensations, emotions, and thought, *but only in order to draw out the essence of the experiences encountered in the preceding incarnation, without having new experiences.*[99] In fact, actual evolution takes place only in the physical plane; in the afterworld, after passing on, evolution consists *simply of summing up, recapitulating and assimilating the experiences that one had in the preceding incarnation. This assimilation happens in the moment when he can put his latest incarnation into relation with the earlier ones that, in some way, are involved in them and have given rise to them. It is thus an assimilation, not an actual evolution. That takes place only in the physical plane.*[100]

It is clear that if the possibility were given to choose between remaining in the astral plane or going back to being reincarnated in the physical plane, the individual would end up trying to escape as much as possible the physical plane – full of pain, toil, and material

---

[99] Florence Circle 77, *Maestro, perché?*, p. 25.
[100] *Ibid.*, p. 101.

problems to be solved – and *seek refuge in that ideal Garden of Eden which the astral plane appears to be.*[101]

The fact that individuals are in the physical plane in order to carry out their evolution is not a matter of choice, but of necessity. For it is only in the material plane that experiences can be lived objectively and responsibly, and ultimately understood.

Once the phase of the *"retreat into one's desires"* has been overcome, in which the individual astrally strips himself of his strongest desires, and of the *"re-examination of one's life,"* the conscience opens its eyes to the real astral world, the true afterlife.

The vision *is something that cannot be described in words: it is a new and marvelous world, made up and shaped by sensations and emotions; the matter of the astral plane has its own special luminosity which is due to the type of elementary unit that makes it up and is highly influenced by the vibrations* (emotions, desires, moods) *of the individuals found in that plane.*[102]

The environment is a constant reproduction of what is known in the physical world. We could say that wherever there are physical mountains, there are astral mountains; where there are physical rivers, there are astral rivers, astral trees and plants, green fields and blue skies.

Alongside all this environment made up of what we could call "objective astral matter," there is a large part of "undifferentiated matter," as though it were in the air, that remains practically free to be modeled at will by the disincarnate souls who live in the astral world.

Immersed in astral nature we can find houses, buildings with the most disparate appearances, landscapes and places desired by the disincarnate – but not with the strong desire that makes them withdraw into themselves – reproduced and shaped by a mere act of will.

In reality, also the "objective astral matter" of the environment and of nature that serves as its background is shaped on the basis of the will of the entities; but these designated entities have such a high degree of evolution and their will succeeds in focusing so intensely and unwaveringly that the vibratory energy they emanate to shape

---

[101] Ifior Circle, *Dall'Uno all'Uno*, vol. III, part II, p. 137.
[102] *Ibid.*, p. 134.

astral matter is capable of creating fixed landscapes that cannot be altered easily, thus they can be considered "objective." The other disincarnate inhabitants, having an evolution that is in any case inferior, can only alter the part of astral matter which has purposely been left "undifferentiated," harmonizing it with the "objective" landscape.

For an inhabitant of the astral world, everything that surrounds him is as real and tangible as physical matter is for a person on Earth. He himself is made up of "alterable" astral matter and can give himself the appearance and age he wants most. In general terms, individuals keep here the same appearance they had on Earth, *but they do not maintain it exactly as they were there, but take on one that is physically more attractive and much younger. This happens if they were already old, while children and young people remain children and young people, but this is pure fiction –* willingly so *– because the soul has no age, ever, and does not become either young or old.*[103]

Habits soon change here: there is no longer the physical necessity to eat or the act of getting dressed, unless one wants to, of course; in that case, to put on some garment, the mere desire is sufficient. Since there is no longer the "routine" of the material world, here life takes on a completely different rhythm: in the astral plane one lives mainly through sensations and emotions. In the physical plane we are used to calculating time, in that every action requires a given amount of time to be completed. Here matter molded by desire makes everything immediate; *it is a sequence of interior events, thus there is a completely different evaluation of succession, the succession analogous to the passage of time in the physical plane. There are no pauses, no empty moments, but everything is a continuous succession of interior events.*[104]

Communication with other inhabitants can take place by emitting sounds with the mouth, but only if one so desires; much more frequently it happens by thought transmission, which is much more convenient and direct.

Moving about, too, does not usually take place in our "habitual" way of walking, since in order to go to some place it is enough to

---

[103] Ennio Sensi, *La vita nei livelli astrali*, Rome, Hermes, 1989, p. 100.
[104] Florence Circle 77, *Maestro, perché?*, p. 29.

want to be in that place, and the transfer happens instantly. So we can imagine how time and space in the afterworld take on a different value indeed compared to the physical plane, even though both of these, time and space, in the astral dimension assume a totally different meaning for the individuals living there.

In the astral world there is a luminosity that pervades everything, but there is no sun to light the day or to mark off the night. In the astral world we could say that it is always daytime; *the various entities that live in those environments, since they do not need to sleep, have no real need for the darkness of night and –* trying to find an equivalent with our climate – *remain in a season with no variation of temperature, living one long and marvelous springtime.*[105]

Colors are more luminous, more vivid. It is as though the light came from inside matter, instead of illuminating it from outside. The chromatic scale is more variegated. In the physical world, the range of reception of vibrations perceptible by the human eye as colors is very limited, while *the astral body's sense can receive a greater range of frequencies. It is as though a radio had the possibility of receiving more than one range of wavelengths. In the same way, there is the possibility of receiving and perceiving colors unthinkable in the physical plane.*[106]

In that particular moment of his existence, when he looks around and observes the astral plane, the individual has the perception of all these different colors and sounds, and has sensations that, unless he has been an evil and cruel person in the broadest sense of the term, are always sensations of great wellbeing, happiness, relaxation, and serenity.[107]

Here we meet our loved ones who passed on before us, just as we shall await the arrival of our loved ones who are still alive. A son or daughter, for example, can meet their parents again, because *time in the astral plane, as a sequence, is not too different from the physical one.*[108] Since the interval of time between the death of the parents and that of their child is short compared to the span of time

---

[105] Sensi, p. 39.
[106] Florence Circle 77, *Maestro, perché?*, p. 34.
[107] *Ibid.*, p. 35.
[108] Ifior Circle, *Morire e vivere*, p. 41.

between one reincarnation and another – which we have seen is on average 350 years – there is the possibility of meeting up again, obviously if there is a desire to do so. It seems obvious, but to encounter a person in the astral plane it is necessary for both of them to have a real desire to meet each other again. If one individual wants to meet another person and the other person likes that idea, in that moment he will feel a sort of pull, and by expressing the same desire himself, the two will meet.

The fable of Abdus

Let's borrow this charming story which appears in the book *Morire e vivere* (Dying and Living) by the Ifior Circle of Genoa.[109] This fable was chosen because its moral embraces what is, in the last analysis, the ultimate goal of evolution, but also because the presumed author of the fable is a big name. I hope you enjoy it.

The night before his sixtieth birthday, Abdus dreamed of his father who, wrapped in white robes, said to him:

"Abdus, my son, the name I gave you means "servant," because I hoped that you would manage to do something useful for others, but instead I see that, up until now – and there are only four days left before your death – you have served only yourself."

With his body trembling and his heart heavy with remorse, suffering, and fear, Abdus woke up; agitated, he got up and went out on the balcony, thinking over his life, while his eyes fell now on the starry sky, now on the rooftops of the city, now on the image of the moon reflected in the pond below him.

When dawn began to fade the stars, Abdus had still not calmed down.

"What have I done for others?" he kept asking himself. "I have spent my life buying, selling, and accumulating money that, after my death, my heirs will squander as fast as they can. But what can I do now to make up for my life, which has consisted of selfishness, greed, and indifference towards those who could not be useful to me? I could give all my wealth to the poor but, accustomed as they are to having nothing, they would waste it immediately and... what if all this has been just a bad dream?"

When the sun finally penetrated the room, Abdus asked himself: "Why do I have to die, anyway? Why do people die?"

---

[109] *Ibid.*, pp. 13-16.

He thought for a while and finally made a decision: he would try to leave other people an answer to this very vexing question.

Early in the morning he went to see the most famous physician in the world, and after having greased well with cash all the doors that led to him, came into the doctor's presence and asked him, "Why do we die?"

The great doctor decided that a person whose pockets were so pleasingly plump could not be a madman and launched into a scholarly explanation of the physiology of death, at the end of which Abdus went his way, asking himself, "Yes, of course... but why?"

The second day he thought that perhaps the right person for him to ask was a priest. Thanks to a generous offering, he gained an audience with the leading religious authority on Earth and asked, "Father, why do we die?"

"My son," he said, "dust thou wert, to dust thou shalt return; love your neighbor as yourself, and by the way, there is a missionary brotherhood that..." Abdus returned home with his morale lower, but his pockets lighter!

The third day he thought that only a philosopher, always accustomed to thinking things through, could have the answer he sought. So he contacted the most highly acclaimed philosopher in the world and, after contributing generously to making sure the man had no other concerns than his meditations, finally he was able to ask, "Why do we die?"

The philosopher rolled his eyes around, assumed a pensive air, stroked his chin, sucked in his lips, and then, after a silence that seemed extremely long to Abdus, murmured, "Why do we live?" He then immediately sank back down into his meditations.

The fourth day he obtained a meeting with the king of logic.

The man who – it was said – had succeeded in demonstrating that the burning of the sun starts from a hair on his dog's tail.

The man asked him for one kilo nine-hundred-ninety-nine grams of pure gold and told him that he needed it as the point of departure to set in motion his logical reasoning in search of the answer Abdus desired. After seven hours and seven minutes, when Abdus was already pricking up his ears to find out if he could hear the first steps of death as it approached him, the great logician stopped a hand mid-air, stared at him, and exclaimed triumphantly, "Why not?"

Abdus returned home as dusk was falling and sat on his balcony with a sad air and an empty stomach because he didn't have a cent left. At the stroke of midnight Abdus saw next to him a girl so marvelous that he was left speechless.

"Who are you?" he finally managed to ask in a tiny voice.

"I am death," the girl answered with a voice like honey.

"If that is true – and I doubt it because you are too beautiful – at least give me an answer to my question," Abdus begged.

Death bent over him, and after touching his chest, mouth, and forehead with icy fingers, whispered, "To learn to live!"

But Abdus would have to wait for a new life.

Ananda / Oscar Wilde.[110]

---

[110] This story is the result of the collaboration between the Guide Ananda and the writer Oscar Wilde, who for a long time appeared to the Ifior Circle using the pseudonym Billy.

The Absolute

It may be that man will never be able to comprehend God, nonetheless this opinion does not exonerate him from meditating on this topic, if for no other reason than to understand that God cannot be.[111]

From the beginning, human beings have tried to conceive of God according to their capacity for interpreting him.

It would be mistaken to imagine from human values the reality of God and on those create a system of ethics: but precisely this error has been made: that is to say, starting from what our senses lead us to believe is reality, human beings have drawn all those conceptions of the divine that make him an anthropomorphic Being, if not in aspect, at least in behavior.[112]

The God of the Catholics, the God of the Protestants, the God of the Jews, the God of any religion is not the God of Reality, he is the God of necessity; he is not the God of infinite love, but the God of hate and love, of good and evil, the God who chastises and rewards, because man needs these relativizations in order to understand eternity. However, if one really wants to perceive the breath of God, it is necessary to move beyond these limitations.[113]

Thus the scientist will speak of God as the great energy and first cause, the theologian will speak of the dogma of the Trinity, the humble peasant will speak of the old man with a beard depicted in churches to whom he must turn to ask for grace and favors when he needs them.

Everyone imagines the God they can construct for themselves, so that it seems like it is more man who creates God in his own

---

[111] Florence Circle 77, *La fonte preziosa*, Rome, Mediterranee, 1987, p. 39.
[112] Florence Circle 77, *Dai mondi invisibili*, p. 217.
[113] Magister, *Voci lontane, vicine presenze*, Cornaredo (MI), Armenia, 2001, p. 199.

image. Now the concept that man has of God is a limitative concept, an anthropomorphic concept.

And so here he falls into that huge error with which the various philosophies struggle even still today, of wanting to place the Creator outside His creation, almost as though He were an aloof, albeit skillful, craftsman of something that He is projecting in front of Him and of which, after having created it, He becomes an attentive witness.

God is not the witness of His creation, He is the creation itself; and this concept – which until not long ago could seem contrary to what religion affirms – today is making its way and becoming more accepted because scientists are realizing more and more that they find this presence everywhere their research penetrates.[114]

In Him everything Is.
Not: "was" or "will be."
Simply: Is.
This means that in the Absolute there is no movement of any sort, there is no flow, there is nothing that changes.

This means that in the Absolute there cannot be anything that is becoming, and that in the Absolute all Reality exists simultaneously with all its characteristics.

You wonder what was there before the Absolute set creation in motion.

If you had truly understood what I just said, you would not ask me this question: in the Absolute there cannot be "before," there cannot be "after," because everything Is, all at the same time.

This means that creation exists in the Absolute already created.

You are the one who, observing it, moving your attention from one element to another of what Is, create, in your perception, the sense of time, of "before" and "after." But, in truth, there does not exist anything that had an existence before or after something else. If this were possible it would mean the existence of something outside of the Absolute, and this would make the Absolute something different from the Absolute itself – since it would not have everything within Itself, it could not be the Absolute.[115]

Absolute: what does this term mean? To understand the concept

---
[114] *Loc. cit.*
[115] Ifior Circle, *Dall'Uno all'Uno,* vol. IV, p. 13.

of Absolute, let's take a very basic example: let's posit, as an absurd hypothesis, that a pen is the only thing existing in the Universe; then there could not exist any material except what makes up a pen. There cannot exist an outside, an external part, otherwise there would be extraneous material besides the pen, and we have said that this cannot exist; there would be no perimeter, otherwise a limit would exist and the limit presupposes something "beyond" the perimeter. Not existing a limit, neither would there exist a form. Our pen, if it were the only thing existing, would be unlimited, infinite, absolute.

Absolute means that nothing else can exist and therefore, according to logic, it has to be immutable.

In the world that you know, any random object that you take into consideration is limited by all the rest that is not that object; that is to say, an object is not alone, existing absolutely. But an object that was like this, that is to say, absolutely the only one that exists, would be unlimited; it would not know the limit of finiteness, it would be infinite.[116]

This is how the Absolute is: It is the only thing that exists, It is infinite, and everything is part of It. God is the galaxy, God is in the atom, in the electron, in cells, in stones. But how can man perceive this divine presence that is in him and everything around him?

We can try to answer this by using a simile. Man, at his stage of evolution, perceives God in the same way as the cell perceives the body that contains it; and yet, in certain moments man manages to sense God's presence inside him.

The more you, on the level of your existence, will feel heightened emotion in coming closer to something that is not you but is other and is outside you, and you are able to appreciate it in its true value, the more you will have regained a part of God that is in you.[117]

---

[116] Florence Circle 77, *La fonte preziosa*, p. 147.
[117] Magister, *Voci lontane, vicine presenze*, p. 214.

Part Two
THE COSMOS

Prologue to Part Two

In the next chapters we try to give a clear, simple explanation of an alternative and innovative model for understanding the universe, matter, and the phenomena that surround humankind.

From the beginning man has tried to comprehend the nature of matter and physical space. For many decades now, scientists have dismissed the hypothesis, accepted in the past ever since the time of Plato,[118] that space, even empty space, was made up of a substance that was invisible, very subtle, and elastic.

The scientists of the nineteenth century, such as Maxwell, Faraday, Fresnel, Herz, and Marconi, attempting to explain phenomena like the transmission of light or electromagnetism, posited that all of existing space was permeated by the same substance. This substance was called *aether*. We shall come upon this term more than once as we continue our discussion.

We shall completely take apart the matter of the physical plane and understand how, going beyond the breakdown of what we shall see is the elementary particle of the physical plane, we arrive at the matter that makes up the dimension immediately after this one: the matter of the soul and of the afterworld.

We discover how aether becomes matter, and understand in a simple manner how phenomena like light, electricity, magnetism, and gravity are produced. And finally, we explore life on other planets and their inhabitants.

---

[118] Plato, *Phaedo*, LVIII.

The planes of existence

Here I want to expand the explanation of the planes of existence by giving some interesting additional information.

In every reincarnation cycle individuals – identified as their conscience – need each time to create for themselves a vehicle suitable for spending time on Earth with their own physical body.

These bodies, as we have already listed, each reside in a different dimension from the others:

- the *physical body*   the seat of action and movement
- the *etheric body*   the seat of vital energy
- the *astral body*   the seat of emotions and desires
- the *mental body*   the seat of thoughts and reasoning

For each plane of existence the individual has vehicles, and for each vehicle or body, senses; but where the senses are muted, the conscience does not operate. This is why you do not perceive much more than what comes into the restricted field of perception of your physical senses.[119]

The conscience, at each incarnation, not only inhabits a new physical body, but needs the contemporary existence of the other related bodies in order to live, and each one of these (physical, etheric, astral, and mental) resides in its own relative plane of existence.

Summarizing what was already discussed in Part One, when the individual comes into this life, his conscience is already aware of all four planes of existence. When he passes on, he immediately abandons the physical body, and shortly afterwards his etheric body also dissolves. The conscience, then, not having any other body available to it, withdraws, manifesting its awareness of living in the body immediately below, that is, the astral one.

---

[119] Florence Circle 77, *Dai mondi invisibili*, p. 141.

So here we are on the threshold of life in the afterworld. But this will not be the definitive stop: after staying here for a more or less long period of time – according to the level of evolution reached – the individual feels the desire to leave the astral plane behind to move on to the mental plane. Here the amount of time spent can be quite long, but not even this plane is the individual's definitive home. Sooner or later the individual will need to leave the mental plane behind too.

The only real home, which never changes with each incarnation, is the plane of the conscience (or the akashic plane). Here the individual will await a new incarnation, and this will entail a new physical, etheric, astral, and mental plane. The physical, etheric, astral, and mental bodies make up the individual's personality, physical appearance, character, expressivity, and way of reasoning: all these together define and form the person's ego. The reason why each new return to life requires a whole set of new bodies is so that the incarnate individual can have different experiences from those in the preceding lifetime, better suited to his new course of evolution.

The following scheme summarizes the cycle of incarnation.

	Body	Plane	Description
The conscience The body is never renewed and receives the experiences had during life	individual conscience	akashic plane	The conscience is the individual's true Reality. It is the only body that does not vary from one life to the next
The ego These bodies are renewed with each incarnation	mental body	mental plane	This is the seat of thought, memory, and reasoning
	astral body	astral plane	This is the seat of emotions, feelings, and desires
	etheric body	etheric plane	This is the seat of vital energy
	physical body	physical plane	This is the seat of action and movement

During birth all the bodies of the ego are created

After passing on, the individual gradually lets go of the bodies of the ego

The physical plane

Among the planes of existence, the physical plane is the only absolutely indispensable plane for learning to evolve.

Only here does the objectivity of matter permit the experiences necessary for the conscience to move forward in its evolution. Only in this plane are the physical laws operative that postulate the consequentiality of cause and effect. Every cause set in action will sooner or later be met by its opposite, corrective effect.

The third principle of motion teaches us that "For every action there is an equal and opposite reaction."[120] Emergency rooms exist to treat the reckless people who learned this lesson the hard way. In this material universe, effect follows cause: if we stick a finger in the fire, it will be burned. Without direct experimentation in the physical plane, the evolution of the conscience would not take even one step forward.

Official science has broken matter down into its smallest components. The Guides of the Florence Circle 77 and the Ifior Circle reveal to us that man will discover what the ancient philosophers of long ago wrote about: the existence of an elementary particle of the physical plane.[121]

This particle, called the "elementary unit," is the ultimate "building block," the smallest one, that forms all of the physical plane. In the chapter on the creation of matter we shall see how the matter of the physical plane is the result of countless aggregations of identical elementary units.

What happens if we try to break this building block down further? What happens is that we no longer obtain physical matter, but astral matter! We will have gone past the threshold of the

---

[120] The third principle of dynamics, known also as Newton's Third Law, can also be expressed formally as follows: "Forces always present themselves in pairs. If Object A exerts a force F on Object B, then Object B will exercise on Object A an equal and opposite force –F."
[121] Plato in *Timaeus* maintained the existence of a sort of very tiny particle on which all matter was based.

physical world and be looking onto the dimension immediately after this one. We will be really observing the matter of the dimension of the *afterworld*.

But this discovery can be made only by means of the conscience; no scientific equipment, no matter how sophisticated, will be able to scrutinize the afterworld, since matter can perceive only what resides in its same material plane.

The elementary unit is nothing other than the connecting link between what you call the visible world and what you define as the invisible world.[122]

In essence, if we took the densest astral matter and aggregated it further with other astral matter, with the aim of creating a new particle, this new particle would not manifest itself still on the astral plane but would become an *elementary unit* of the physical plane, thus creating the material dimension.

From where, then, does all the energy derive which suffuses the physical plane and enables the incessant movement of the stars and of physical life?

Energy, as we shall see, is nothing other than the vibration of the elementary unit. And the elementary unit vibrates because the matter underneath it vibrates: the energy of physical matter comes from the vibration of astral matter.

For us "pure energy" is "matter of the astral plane," that is to say, that which is obtained from the disintegration of the most elementary physical matter.[123]

The elementary unit in and of itself and lacking the input of vibration would be inert, and as a result there would be no energy; and since we have stated that this is the ultimate form of matter of the physical plane indivisible into other physical matter, it follows that what makes it vibrate, which is what gives it energy, does not belong to and does not come from the physical plane.

This can be sufficient to postulate at least another plane of existence beyond the physical one, from which necessarily must come the cause – the energy – that generates the first vibration of your plane.[124]

---

[122] Ifior Circle, *Dall'Uno all'Uno,* vol. III, part I, p. 33.
[123] Florence Circle 77, *Dai mondi invisibili*, p. 198.
[124] Ifior Circle, *Dall'Uno all'Uno*, vol. III, part I, p. 50.

The etheric plane

The etheric body of every living being functions as the interface between the physical and the astral bodies. It governs and channels the vital energies and regulates the individual's immune defenses and state of health in general. The etheric body also plays another role: it acts so to speak as the matrix, the mold which will shape the physical body as it grows. Because of its special function as a morphological and anatomical model, from which the physical body will develop its copying process, it is also known as the *etheric double*. From the semantic point of view, the term "etheric double" means that it is the exact duplicate of the dense body, but in a rarer matrix.

In reality the *etheric plane* is not a plane of existence strictly speaking, but only a particular *subtle* state of physical matter that acts as an intermediary with astral matter, and is thus not a place – in the sense of a dimension – where the conscience can manifest itself and live.

The etheric body is still physical matter but in a much more rarefied state. It is nothing other than a certain vibratory state of the elementary unit, of the *aether*. It receives energies directly from the astral plane and channels them by interfacing with the physical plane.

The etheric body is closely tied to the physical body, actually being an integral part of it.

During a person's lifetime these two bodies – physical and etheric – remain always close to each other, so much so that the vital manifestation of every living creature is indissolubly tied to the existence of its etheric double. This rarely reaches the point of breaking away – except when it is a sign of some illness or bio-physical imbalance – since this separation is never a positive development. However, the separation can be forced; it is possible to elicit artificially the temporary distancing of the etheric body. This occurs, for example, with anesthesia.

In fact, when you anesthetize a person, if you need to for surgery, with the anesthetics you do nothing more than separate away the etheric body; the connection between the dense physical body and the astral body is interrupted, and the creature no longer perceives pain, which originates in the dense physical body.

This can be understood by knowing that the etheric body is still physical, albeit at a subatomic level, thus it can be influenced by a physical substance, by a dense material like an anesthetic; yet all this would be incomprehensible and indeed absurd if I had said that using an anesthetic you send away the astral body, which is matter, in its essence, much finer than physical matter, which can therefore not be influenced by dense physical matter.[125]

Even when the etheric body is distanced – artificially, through a near-death experience[126] or sometimes during sleep – it still stays connected to the physical body through what we could call a silvery white thread attached to the body; in practice it is the etheric body itself that, as it is pulled away, stretches leaving a thin thread that can be extended practically infinitely: this is the so-called "*Silver Cord.*"

A different mechanism comes into play during sleep.

Everyone will have had the experience sometimes of waking up suddenly with a pounding heart and the unpleasant sensation of dreaming that we are falling into a pit. It wasn't a dream...

What happened was that while the body was fast asleep, the astral one wandered off in its own realms; then suddenly something disturbed the body, causing a sudden awakening. There was no process of the usual signals of normal waking up, and so the astral had to "re-enter" brusquely. This is translated by the brain into a bad dream.[127]

In the entire physical body of every individual there are thousands and thousands of tiny points which are predisposed to receive and transmit the vibrations between the physical and the astral planes.[128]

---

[125] Florence Circle 77, *Maestro, perché?*, p. 55.
[126] *NDE* is the abbreviation for *Near Death Experience.*
[127] Dembech Giuditta, *L'ultimo Tabù*, Turin, Ariete Multimedia, 2009, p. 47.
[128] Ifior Circle, *Morire e vivere*, p. 72, par. 1.

These tiny points – called *"nadis"* (from the Sanskrit meaning "channel") have two characteristics:

- They have the task of keeping the physical body joined to the astral body. In a certain sense they act as a magnet;
- They serve to transmit the vibrations that arrive from the astral and the other planes of existence. Remember that the vibrations are what we call *energies*.

The *nadis* emit *electromagnetic vibrations*[129] and are manifested on the physical plane as *bioelectric* effects that can be detected scientifically.

Modern science, too, states that every action of the physical body, from muscles to cells to nerves, is invariably accompanied by a corresponding electrical action. The cell has an electrical potential – known as *membrane potential* – on an average around -70mV (millivolts)[130] and can vary according to the state of health of the cell itself. This is well known to modern medicine, to the point that various studies have been completed recently for the early diagnosis of cancer using bioelectric signals, by identifying the cells that can turn themselves into tumors.[131]

The *nadis* are like tiny vortexes of energy distributed along the entire nervous system of the individual, even into the smallest nerves of the peripheral system. In the points of the etheric body where the flows of energy of the *nadis* intersect with others many times as they flow, scattered throughout the body, a multitude of larger energy centers form, as though the vortexes of the *nadis* grouped together into larger vortexes. Among these, there are seven major energy centers which are larger than all the others: these are known as *chakras* (from the Sanskrit for "circle"). The seven *chakras* are located vertically along the spine and correspond physically to the main glands of the endocrine system and reflexively to specific organs of the physical body. The chakras can

---

[129] *Ibid.*, p. 72, par. 2.
[130] See Luciano Vella, *Enciclopedia Medica Italiana - Aggiornamento II Edizione*, Florence, USES Edizioni Scientifiche, 1993, p. 6025.
[131] See Brook T. Chernet and Michael Levin, "Transmembrane voltage potential is an essential cellular parameter for the detection and control of tumor development in a Xenopus model", *Disease Models & Mechanisms*, 2013 (http://dmm.biologists.org/content/6/3/595).

be compared to large energy vortexes into which a great quantity of energy flows from the other planes of existence.

Nadis and *chakras* together (plus a multitude of other lesser energy vortexes) make up the etheric body which, in its visual and chromatic aspect, corresponds to a person's so-called *aura*.

The aura is the nebulous and at the same time luminous form which clairvoyants see around the physical body of human beings, and also of animals or plants.[132]

The aura can take on various colorations according to the individual's state of health or mood, and clairvoyants – authentic ones – who have this real ability to actually see the aura can also identify and, if they have acquired a certain amount of familiarity and experience, diagnose possible health problems; this is due to the fact that health problems, even before they reveal themselves as illness in the physical body, manifest themselves as an energy imbalance in the etheric body.

An illness can be detected in the etheric body weeks or even months before it is manifested in the dense physical body.

The etheric body vibrates and stays alive in that it receives vibratory energy from the astral body and to a lesser degree from the other planes of existence: the mental and akashic.

We know, however, that everything in the cosmos achieves equilibrium as the result of two forces that act, one from the inside and the other from the outside.

We have, however, always said that every input is dual: one comes from outside and the other from inside.[133]

From where does the external counterpart of energy come? From our sun!

The sun, as we know from science, emanates the entire spectrum of electromagnetic waves. Solar radiation encompasses – according to wavelength – radio waves, microwaves, infrared rays, ultraviolet (UV) rays, X-rays, gamma rays, and cosmic rays. But in the entire solar spectrum a much more subtle type of vibration is also emanated. This is what Indians call *prana* ("life" in Sanskrit). *Prana* in essence is nothing other than a particular vibration of the elementary unit, just as is any other solar emanation.

---

[132] Florence Circle 77, *Per un mondo migliore*, pp. 203-204.

[133] Florence Circle 77, *Dai mondi invisibili*, p. 199.

This explains also the fact that *prana* is present in greater quantities on sunny days. Practically speaking, the more intense the sunlight, the more *prana* we receive.

Prana, abundant during the daytime, is present in any case also after sunset and during the night, even if in significantly lesser quantities. This could seem absurd, given that *prana*, traveling at the speed of light like all the electromagnetic waves, in the absence of sunlight should follow the same fate as visible light: it should disappear.

In reality, just as the photons of light bond with physical matter in the form of heat – we know that the photons make atoms vibrate faster, and this can be detected as an increase in temperature – *prana* too bonds with matter, especially with the atoms making up the air we breathe, making it vibrate in a more subtle and detectable form, no longer as heat, but as vital energy.

It is no coincidence that the foods that are healthier – from the scientific and nutritional standpoints – are the ones that have been under the effect of the sun's rays the longest and that can be consumed just as they are, without the losses resulting from cooking, i.e., fruits and vegetables.

When we eat, the material part of food nourishes the material part of the body, while *prana* nourishes the etheric part, recharging it. This process of recharging takes place because the vibrations of the etheric body and of *prana* have the same identical frequency, so that, added together, the result is a more intense vibration; to make an analogy, when we strike or pluck a stretched cord it vibrates even more rapidly.

The etheric body, once recharged, will have more energy to distribute to the physical body, starting from an increase in the immune system.

Most food is absorbed by human beings not because life has as an essential condition that of absorbing a large amount of dense physical matter; but mainly, the individual extracts prana, vital energy, from food.

The physical vehicle can be kept alive without ingesting great amounts of food, by taking in prana also from water, the air, and sunlight.

Everything that is exposed to the light has a greater content of prana than what is, on the contrary, far away from it.[134]

From this we can deduce that the time of day when *prana* is most abundant for man's benefit is sunset, since the air has been able to accumulate the maximum amount of *prana* available to it during the day.

Pranic breathing is most efficacious at the time of sunset, since there was sunlight all day long. The percentage of prana diminishes during the night.[135]

To conclude this chapter, let us see how the etheric body is abandoned.

At the moment of death, with the abandonment of the physical body the astral body detaches from the physical body. Thus the etheric body, no longer receiving the energy necessary to feed it, slowly dissolves and is dispersed into the surrounding environment, going back to being an *elementary unit* in the resting state.

Concretely speaking, the tiny vortexes – the *nadis* – begin to slow their vibration, gradually ceasing to function. It is as though electrically they gradually turned off. They do not stop immediately, since they still continue to receive energy from the physical plane, from the *prana* of the sun.

This phase of dissolution of the etheric double lasts an average of 36 hours after clinical death, a period in which the deceased individual still feels tied in some way to its physical body and the Earthly world. After that, the soul is totally unleashed from the material dimension, and the conscience finds itself living once again in the astral world.

---

[134] Florence Circle 77, *Maestro, perché?*, pp. 165-167.
[135] *Ibid.*, p. 166.

The astral plane

The astral plane is the place where the individual's astral body lives, moves, and governs itself. On a theological level, the astral plane coincides with the *afterworld* and the relative astral body with the *soul*.

In the chapter "Life in the Afterworld," we spoke exhaustively of life in the astral plane. After a short summary, in this chapter we'll look at the mechanisms that shape astral matter.

The astral plane is the plane that governs sensations, emotions, and desires. It is here that the relative matter of our astral body vibrates when we laugh, cry, are happy, angry, or frightened. It is here that the conscience develops its desires, which it will experience – karma permitting – in the physical plane. The astral world, like the physical world, has a place of manifestation, an atmosphere, and an environment in which to live.

The matter of the astral plane has a very interesting characteristic: it can be molded by the mere impulse of the will and desire. All that is necessary is to want an object, a food, or anything else our heart desires and instantly the astral matter assumes the perfect form of the expressed wish.

What is the element that enables this apparent "miracle"? It is always *vibration*. The individual's astral body, in the act of expressing its desire, does nothing other than make the matter around it vibrate. Just as in the physical plane the energy of the action, following the law of cause and effect, sets the elementary unit to vibrating, so in the astral plane the energy of the desire sets the relative astral elementary unit to vibrating. This is because *given that astral matter is much smaller than physical matter, it follows that a vibration which on the physical plane collides with physical matter without provoking short-term changes in it, on the astral plane easily elicits a change in the internal cycles of the astral matter and thus a more immediate change in its form.*[136]

Of course, on the physical plane the energy put into a desire is not sufficient to transform the surrounding matter into – I don't know – an ice-cream cone! To do this it is necessary for the desire to have the intermediation and support of the energy of the relative plane: it is necessary to complete the action, to act in some way, otherwise the desired ice-cream cone does not "materialize"!

On the astral plane, things are different: there the desire and emotions are sufficient by themselves, as vibration, to set in motion changes in the astral matter.[137]

When a person is incarnate and has a physical body, does our astral body then have any influence over matter? Not exactly, or to put it better: there is no other matter besides our physical body. The stronger a desire or an emotion we feel, the stronger will be the corresponding vibration of our astral body. The astral body is connected – remember? – with the physical body through the "interface" of the etheric body. The astral body needs this interface in order to dialogue with the physical body, since the astral is not matter of the physical plane and would have no way of communicating if there were not this "intermediate" matter.

Now, the strong vibration deriving from a sudden emotional state, such as a burst of anger, pours down from the astral body – the source of the anger – first to our etheric body, the one responsible for our state of energy and health.

The etheric body, being directly connected on a physical level to our body's various hormonal glands,[138] by reaction will immediately activate chemical reactions in a series of hormones which will do nothing other than emphasize that particular mood, among other things not really beneficial but probably necessary to the person in order to have a certain type of experience. The stronger the desire, the more astral matter we will shape. But how is a desire born?

A person's desire does not originate in the astral body – as one might reflexively think – but derives from his akashic body. It is the conscience that manifests the need to know something which it has not yet understood or to go more deeply into a topic that is not yet clear.

---

[136] Ifior Circle, *Dall'Uno all'Uno,* vol. III, part I, p. 144.
[137] *Ibid.*, p. 145.
[138] See the chapter "Life in the Afterworld."

The vibration that will derive from this need, starting from the akashic plane and crossing the subplanes, will be transformed in the astral plane into desire.

In other words, the conscience, by manifesting its need, sets the mental plane to vibrating, which the individual will perceive as a strong fixation, and in turn this insistent thought will cause the astral body to vibrate, definitively manifesting the need by means of the desire.

And the stronger the conscience's need, the more intense its vibration will be and the more strongly the desire will spring forth.

Someone who lives in the afterworld can see the plane below – the physical world – simply by desiring to do this, but they cannot interact with it because they cannot be seen or heard.

The inhabitant of the astral plane, on the other hand, cannot observe the mental world, since that is a higher plane than his, in the same way that an inhabitant of the physical world cannot see the plane above him, the afterworld.

Often, very often, someone living in the afterworld does not know or is literally ignorant of the existence of dimensions above him, to the point of believing he has arrived in the paradise he was waiting for and that he will stay there *forever*.

"Forever" is an infinite and indefinite time, but we can say that, in accordance with an individual's evolution, he can stay in the afterworld for hundreds and hundreds of years, in terms of the passage of physical time. In any case he *always* stays there as long as he has a strong desire to do so, never because of constraint or other external factors.

At the point that he feels the need to go beyond this, the desire to continue his journey of exploration – once again it is desire that gives the command – will make him abandon, like old clothes, his astral body, which will then dissolve.

The conscience will now be at the gates of the mental world.

The mental plane

The dimension of the mental plane is the seat of the individual's thought and reasoning. Just as in the astral plane it is desire that makes the object materialize, in the mental plane thought is sufficient to have the immediate sensation of a real contact between us and the object of our thought. Here too the reason is simple: in the mental plane the elementary unit is enormously smaller than in the astral plane, so that it does not even need an effort of will or emotional impulse of desire to shape the surrounding environment. For the matter of the mental plane is thought.

The mental plane is also the site of memory. Memory is a particular, denser aggregation of the vibration of the elementary unit of the mental plane, just as solid matter is in the physical plane. From this we can intuit that, for today's scientist or medical doctor, looking in the human brain for the origin of thought is like taking apart a television set to seek in the electronic components the movie that was broadcast. The brain is only a means designated to receive and adapt, using physical filters, what comes in from other planes of existence. The study, further investigation, and repetition of concepts during a person's lifetime have precisely the function of reinforcing the vibration of the mental plane, as though thought received new vibratory energy in order to memorize the cognitive notion.

As incarnate beings – as persons alive on Earth – study is really the training ground of the mental plane. When, as disincarnate beings – after passing on – we have reached the point of living with the conscience in the mental plane, we will have the possibility, with no effort whatsoever, of *arriving at knowing everything that was known in the past, with the aid of the mere impulse of the desire to know.*

It is evident that also in this plane the impulse to act is supplied by desire and therefore by the needs of the akashic body (the conscience); *without this the individual would not move and the life of his bodies on the various planes would be extremely static.*[139]

The mental world, too, has its own atmosphere and environment in which to live *consciously* and to encounter those who have already arrived there in the course of their evolution, after having left behind, *of their own free will*, the astral world.

One does not reach the mental world *by the death* of the astral body, but because the individual has reached a point in his personal journey where he no longer feels the need to stay in the astral plane. The astral shell melts away and in an instant the new mental environment opens up before the conscience.

Also those who live in the mental world can see in any case the planes below – i.e., the astral and physical – but cannot interact with them, since the individual does not have sufficient mental energy to make the matter vibrate, first of the astral and then of the physical plane, unless he is an entity with a very high degree of evolution.

---

[139] Ifior Circle, *Dall'Uno all'Uno,* vol. III, part I, p. 176.

The akashic plane (the conscience)

The physical, etheric, astral, and mental planes are also called *the planes of the I*, in that their relative bodies are specifically created at every incarnation and constitute the personality and physical makeup of the individual on Earth; and we have learned that these are bit by bit sloughed off by the individual at the end of each lifetime.

The akashic body, on the other hand, always remains and is never left behind or regenerated from one lifetime to the next. It exists forever because it has to accumulate the evolutive essence of all the experiences one has had in past lives.

It is this plane that we have always indicated as the seat of the individual conscience, which is built up progressively as the individual, becoming incarnate, has experiences. In the conscience is summarized the life of the whole person, just as in the brain is summarized the life of the whole physical body.[140]

In fact, what has been experienced and learned during the various incarnations is never lost, but persists inside the individual's akashic body. And above all, the essence of those experiences persists in the form of understandings that the conscience was lacking before, and that are essential for the constitution and expansion of the conscience itself, and consequently for its evolution.

We should not think of the akashic plane – or the mental plane – as a cold dimension, as if the conscience were wandering in an empty atmosphere. Every plane has its own environment and its "inhabitants," its time and space, even if these are substantially different between one plane and another.

The mechanism by which the conscience, in expressing its evolutionary needs, crosses all the planes of existence, is the following: the conscience (in the akashic plane) at the moment

---

[140] Florence Circle 77, *Oltre l'illusione*, p. 201.

when it expresses the desire to reach the point of understanding an aspect in which it is deficient, as a first step implements a logical thought, a reasoning compatible with its morality, creating vibrations in the mental body. But the thought, as it becomes more pressing and dense, becomes a desire, thus shaping the astral body. The desire, finally, in order to become manifest for the purpose of satisfying the ego, becomes an action in the material plane. From here it will receive as feedback a reaction to the cause set in motion which, retracing the planes in the opposite direction, will reach the akashic plane as the essence of the experience just lived.

So then, all the bodies become nothing other than vehicles for learning, used by the individual conscience to *know itself* for the purpose of evolving. At the end of each incarnation, they are cast aside as worn-out tools.

Critique of classical evolutionism

Darwinian evolutionism is a subject that even today is very hard to discuss, since it is taught in schools and scientific circles as untouchable dogma. Evolutionism is the view – more philosophical than scientific – that the living universe is in constant evolution from imperfect forms to increasingly perfect forms, and human beings and animals are the product of billions and billions of genetic mutations, starting even from inert matter to arrive at living matter, and from less complex living beings to more complex ones.

Darwin's theory of evolution starts from a refutation of the fixity of species to affirm that life moved from one animal species to another, arriving finally at the human species. Science, thanks to technological processes of the most recent decades, has by now decreed that it is not possible to exchange genetic characteristics between different species. The discovery of DNA has verified this thesis, demonstrating in the laboratory that DNA is a genetically stable structure. A causal modification in DNA is not possible in terms of evolution, because mutations are all deleterious, leading to spontaneous abortions, malformations, and degenerative pathologies of various sorts. If we exclude induced mutations (which are also always negative, such as those caused by carcinogenic substances or radiation), our genetic heritage does not undergo variations transmittable to following generations that maintain a memory of the life lived. Scientifically, it is possible to transform only secondary characteristics, but never to change from one species to another.

Modifications within the same species exist – the only ones possible – and are called microevolution. Conversely, macroevolution, that is to say passing from one species to another, is absolutely impossible.

There do not exist in nature intermediate species that are evolving into something else. Fossils have never been found that could bear witness to the presence of intermediate links between mammals which are very different from each other or between extremely different species like reptiles and mammals. In essence, if evolution between species had truly taken place, the Earth would be full of billions of fossils of these transitory forms. Not even one sole fossil of this type exists. Not only that, but there does not even exist a logic that justifies why a worm should be "better" than a snake or a human being. Morphologically, every being is perfect for the environment in which it lives.

How could inert matter give origin to living matter? For evolutionists the answer is: by chance. And yet, I am not so sure that leaving a dismantled watch in a box and waiting a few million years, between an Earthquake and a monsoon, someone could in the end find the watch accidentally put back together and, what is more, fully functioning!

The hypothesis of the *self-generation of life* has been considered scientifically ridiculous by many of today's scientists. As we can experience in everyday reality, chance generates only chaos.

DNA, in its unceasing process of synthesizing and building, is the most stable structure in the universe. Indeed, when external factors cause DNA to mutate by chance, scientific studies attribute those mutations to the rise of degenerative diseases due to the increase in rare alleles in the DNA.[141] And we are speaking of the same casual mutations that according to Darwin's theory of evolution should be at the origin of new species.

For example, science has shown that giraffes did not get long necks from a genetic mutation for the purpose of gaining an evolutionary advantage for procuring food; it is because they have a complicated, purpose-built internal circulatory system that permits them not to die from not enough blood going to their brain, something that would happen if the neck lengthened by chance.

The complexity of living organisms is such that it impossible that there is no design behind it, and thus a designer. So then, what came first, the chicken or the egg? Prepare yourselves for the right answer: what came first is the *etheric matrix*! This is the true seat

---

[141] See E. Pennetta, "Neodarwinismo alla 'deriva': la speciazione allopatrica conduce all'estinzione," in *Critica Scientifica*, May 2012; A. Keinan and A.G. Clark, "Recent Explosive Human Population Growth Has Resulted in an Excess of Rare Genetic Variants", *Science,* 2012, vol. 336, Issue 6082, pp. 740-743.

and administrator of vital energy, not matter. And even before this came the astral matrix, and before that the mental.

Life proceeds always in order of the planes of existence, never in the opposite direction. It will never happen that a species manifests itself as the result of a genetic, and therefore physical, mutation, but it manifests because the mutation is "pushed" and urged on by passing first through the mental body, then the astral body, and then by creating the etheric body suitable for it, finally causing the birth of the more or less different physical body, which the researcher will see and classify as a "genetic mutation."

In reality, it is not that the species mutates in that it has evolved, but what has changed is the evolution of the creature; it required a body a bit less rough than the preceding one in order to carry out the experiences and discoveries that will enrich evolution once again in the akashic plane.

Although it might seem very unusual, the perspective for looking at evolution has to be overturned: it is not the physical plane that sets in motion the process of evolution, but a need on the body's part for new experiences necessary from one lifetime to the next.

The expanding Earth

Official science today teaches us that the heart of the Earth is a liquid core with an extremely high temperature made up mainly of molten iron and nickel. Like a dynamo, as the Earth turns the iron core creates the planet's magnetic field. Nonetheless, the center of the Earth is too hot for metal magnetism. Beyond a temperature of 770°C any ferromagnetic mineral loses its magnetic properties. This crucial temperature is known as the *Curie point*. And this raises serious doubts about how the Earth's magnetism can derive from the planet's iron core.

Now let's talk about continental drift: today's interpretation operates according to the official model of "tectonic plates." In the course of history, as we know, a great continent (Pangea) broke apart, forming the Earth's current configuration. For some time now, however, a growing number of geologists and scientists are harboring doubts about the process of plate tectonics and the internal composition of the core. Let's go into the question more deeply.

In the early twentieth century the formulation of an alternative theory for the formation of the continents began to take shape: this was "expansion tectonics," in which it was postulated for the first time that the diameter of the Earth does not remain constant over time, but is constantly expanding. The new theory was formulated after various observations – which we shall look at in a moment – hypothesizing an expansion of the globe at the rate of some tens of millimeters per year. All the geological, geographical, and geophysical data used to prove both the theory of *plate tectonics* and that of *expansion tectonics* are identical. The only reason why fifty years ago plate tectonics prevailed lies, quite rightly, in the fact that scientists were faced with the impossibility of justifying and verifying scientifically how matter, necessary to make the globe grow larger, could be created internally. Since then, technology has made great progress – from satellite technology to data processing – just as science has progressed in the understanding of the physical Earth and the principles of global tectonics.

As early as 1889 the Italian scientist Roberto Mantovani presented the hypothesis of expansion.[142] He supposed that one sole continent covered the surface of an Earth which at the time was smaller. As a result of volcanic activity, Earth grew; then that continent broke apart into numerous pieces which moved apart from each other, with the oceans filling in the breaks. Various researchers, such as Prof. Samuel Warren Carey (1911-2002) of the University of Tasmania and Dr. James Maxlow (1949-), just to mention two, have devoted their studies and efforts to bringing to the attention of science the proof, by now certain, that Earth is expanding.

Dr. Maxlow, actively involved in spreading and defending the merits of the theory of terrestrial expansion with lectures in Japan, Greece, and Australia, maintains that Earth currently grows at the rate of 22 millimeters per year. He has analyzed the rising of the seafloor in the central Atlantic Ocean (known as the "mid-ocean ridge") and has observed, using magnetic instruments (magnetometers), that basalt, the iron-rich volcanic rock which makes up the ocean floor, presents alternating magnetic polarities, like "zebra" stripes, arranged in parallel rows (figs. 3 and 4).

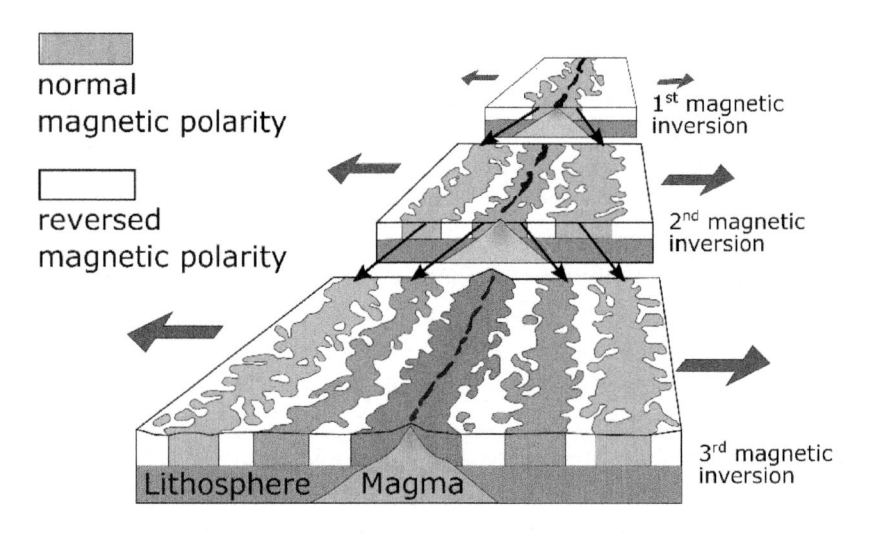

Fig. 3 – Parallel magnetic stripes along the mid-ocean ridge in the Atlantic

---

[142] See Roberto Mantovani, "Le fratture della crosta terrestre e la teoria di Laplace," in *Bull. Soc. Sc. et Arts Réunion*, 1889, pp. 41-53.

During the mapping of the seafloor, carried out in the 1950s by a team of scientists and geologists using repurposed aerial magnetic instruments designed during World War II, they discovered that these magnetic anomalies were not an isolated or chance phenomenon; this pattern was later labeled "magnetic striping." They discovered that along the "rupture" of this ridge the seafloor lavas are much younger, and their age increases the farther away they are from the crest of the ridge.

The stripes of rock parallel to the ridge have been shown to have alternating magnetic polarity (normal-reverse-normal, etc.) indicating that in the course of history the Earth's magnetic field has changed direction numerous times. Science, too, confirms that this has happened dozens of times. The inversion seems to follow cycles of 600,000 to 700,000 years. The theory of plate tectonics presumes that the Earth's radius has remained essentially constant over time. But when new volcanic lava is injected along the axes of expansion of the mid-ocean ridge, the seafloor spreads, enabling the formation of new, more recent crust; this increase in the surface of the seafloor is a clear and unequivocal reflection of the increase in the radius of the Earth.

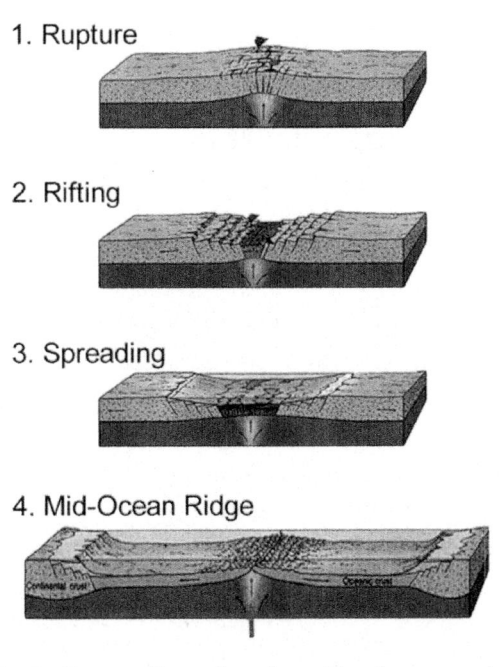

1. Rupture

2. Rifting

3. Spreading

4. Mid-Ocean Ridge

Fig. 4 – Structurally weak seafloor ridge that opens along the mid-ocean crest to form a new ocean

What is more, it should be emphasized that exactly the same crustal fragments that make up both the ancient supercontinents and today's continents can be fitted together, in a sort of spherical puzzle, onto an Earth with a smaller radius to form one single supercontinent.[143]

Mere coincidence?

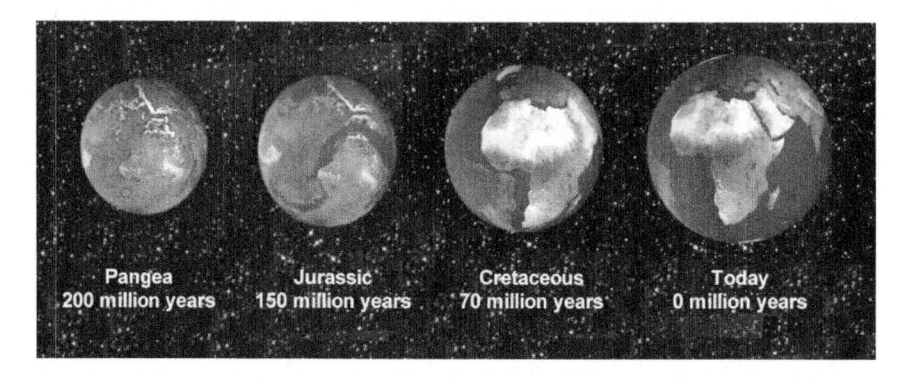

Fig. 5 – Growth in size of the Earth from Pangea to today, with evidence of the process of "expansion tectonics"

Currently, many researchers fervently hope for acceptance of expansion tectonics as the plausible tectonic process, since by now the scientific evidence supporting it is clear. The only thing necessary now is an updating of recent scientific literature.

This is not all of the evidence in favor of expansion tectonics, or even all of the surprises. From this theory we have learned that Earth was originally smaller, with a diameter estimated at about half the current one. This assertion brings with it the supposition that gravity, too, originally was significantly less strong!

This evidence would be sufficient to explain the massive size of dinosaurs, as well as the dimensions of over one meter of certain dragonfly fossils; it is due to the fact that they would have had the benefit of a lesser gravitational pull in the past. The size of

---

[143] See (in Italian) James Maxlow, "Panoramica sulla tettonica di espansione della Terra", *Nexus* no. 86, June-July 2010, p. 39; see also http://www.jamesmaxlow.com/magnetic-sea-floor-mapping.

dinosaurs has always been an enigma that needed solving; in the laws of physics, the proportion of mass to size to strength has to respect specific ratios, and this exigency raises more than one question.

Recently Theodore Holden has examined the ratio between size, weight, and strength of animals and has brought up the question again.[144] The resistance of muscle tissue is fairly constant from one animal species to another. Strength, in relation to weight, imposes a limit on massive dimensions. Holden's calculations indicate that this limit is approached in today's heaviest elephants; this means that, with the current force of gravity, an elephant is the largest size that any animal form can take. Beyond this size, the animal's musculature would not be sufficient to hold it up.

The evolution of pterodactyls is shrouded in mystery about how they could fly, given their size and the conformation of their legs, which did not permit them to take flight as birds do today. The largest dinosaurs were many times larger than an elephant. Moreover, dinosaur skeletons are not even structured well enough to support their weight, while those of elephants are.[145]

How can this be? The limit on size depends on weight, and weight depends on the force of gravity. Earth during the Mesozoic Era had a diameter and a gravity that were less than they are today.

All well and good. So, if our planet has increased in diameter, from where does all this mass come? From where was the matter taken?

The Russian engineer and astronomer Ivan Osipovich Yarkovsky, in 1888, attempting to formulate a new explanation of gravity, created a theory based on the stream of aether. According to his hypothesis, the celestial bodies absorb aether and their mass increases.[146] His theory intended to demonstrate that aether and matter[147] are two different states of the same entity.

---

[144] See Theodore Albon Holden, *Dinosaurs, Gravity, and Changing Scientific Paradigms*, Bear Fabrique, 2004
(http://www.bearfabrique.org/FBook_Utube_Materials/gravity_PastAges.pdf).
[145] See Laurent Sacco, "*Les dinosaures étaient moins massifs qu'on ne le pensait*", Futura Planète, 3/7/2009.
[146] See Ivan Osipovich Yarkovsky, *Ipotesi cinetica della Gravitazione universale e connessione con la formazione degli elementi chimici*, 1888.
[147] The aether, it must be kept in mind, is the matrix of the physical plane made up

Numerous other researchers, like Schappeller, Searl, and Roschin, have demonstrated in the laboratory that the creation of new matter is closely correlated with the creation, under particular magnetic bonds, of an etheric plasma.

Earth's core is not made up of molten iron, but is a mass of matter in the etheric plasma state, which manifests the phenomena known as magnetic fields and gravitational force. It is as though at the center of the Earth there were a little sun!

What is plasma in the etheric state? This question will be answered in the next chapter, after we have discussed the characteristics which official science still ignores about our sun.

---

of elementary units. It is the "supporting foundation" of matter. It is comparable to the modern concept of "quantum void" or what Einstein called "field."

The Sun

In today's scientific knowledge, the sun is defined as a sphere of plasma at a very high temperature. Current science attributes to the sun the capacity to transmit various types of energy to emanate electromagnetic rays, the flow of particles and neutrinos. Let's go now into closer detail, adding information contained in messages received by the Florence Circle 77.[148]

Internally, the sun resembles more the matter of the astral plane, pure energy. It is a point of passage between pure energy and the matter of the physical plane; by slowing its vibration, the sun makes the matter of the astral plane become an elementary unit of the physical plane. This process literally "creates" matter. The sun can thus be compared to a sort of hole in the physical plane – the opposite of a black hole – that puts the physical plane into communication with the astral plane.

What we see of the sun is nothing but an outer shell.

Internally, the sun is in a very different state from matter. Internally, the sun is not hot. It cannot be, because there is no physical matter. There are not, as is commonly thought, rapidly vibrating atomic nuclei. The phenomenon of high temperature concerns only the outer layer, that sort of shell which we can see. That is all that is really very hot.

We know that the sun emanates a wide range of vibrations, the entire spectrum of electromagnetic waves, from light to ultraviolet to gamma rays. But the sun emits above all particles in the elementary state, that is to say elementary units of the physical plane.

This is how matter becomes manifested. The sun, emanating elementary units and setting them into more and more complex vibrations, reproduces the creative mechanism which we shall examine in detail in the chapter on the creation of matter.

---

[148] See Florence Circle 77, *Maestro, perché?*, p. 189.

Every revolutionary theory has always been considered inadmissible in the beginning – this is inevitable. Just like the prediction that the center of the Earth, too, is an etheric plasma, the same as the sun but on a reduced scale. Thanks to this constant contribution of matter from the astral plane, Earth has been able to grow constantly in size, since its core is continually supplied new astral energy, which is transformed into new elementary units of the physical plane. This hypothesis gives concrete form to the missing link of "tectonic expansion."

There are surprises in store also concerning the origin of the gravitational force of the sun and the Earth, but we shall speak of this in the chapter on gravity.

Life on other planets and extraterrestrials

The Universe is teeming with life everywhere. By now this is affirmed by a great many scientific studies, among them, just to mention one, the recent publication in the journal *Astrobiology* by scientists at the University of Rochester and the University of Washington[149] on the past and present existence of advanced extraterrestrial civilizations. Scientists are more or less unanimous in considering it illogical and absurd to say that "we are alone in the universe."

In our galaxy, the Milky Way (fig. 6), there are nine billion solar systems similar to our own.

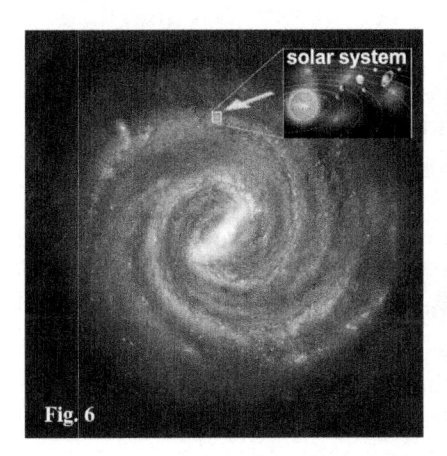

Fig. 6

Fig. 7

The image in figure 7, taken by the Hubble space telescope, shows a small portion of the universe, which is made up of two trillion galaxies.[150] Eighteen thousand billions of billions of solar

---

[149] Frank A., Sullivan W.T., "A New Empirical Constraint on the Prevalence of Technological Species in the Universe", *Astrobiology Journal*, May 2016, New York, Mary Ann Liebert, Inc., 2016.
[150] See Christopher J. Conselice, A. Wilkinson, K. Duncan, A. Mortlock, University of Nottingham UK, "The evolution of galaxy number density at z<8 and its implications", *The Astrophysical Journal*, October 2016.

systems, each of them containing an equal number of hypothetical inhabitable planets like Earth, just to give an idea.

Evolution on other planets, on other worlds that host organized forms of life like that of human beings, even if arranged differently, is analogous and has the same aim of enlarging and enriching the conscience through analogous experiences.[151]

In each solar system, one and only one planet at a time is inhabited. In your system, for example, the Earth is the only planet that currently hosts a form of life, not only on the vegetable and animal levels, but also on the human level.[152]

Leaving aside the details that might seem borrowed from science fiction, we can maintain without a shadow of doubt, given the quantity of messages and confirmations, that the purpose of life on other planets is the same as that on Earth: to develop the evolution of the conscience of individuals who are born there, through experiences acquired in their repeated incarnations and the gradual abandonment of the self-centered ego.

Their physical characteristics can be very different from those of human beings: just as the color of their skin could be much lighter or much darker or tend towards a substantially different color; they could be tall and slim, more slender or more stocky according to their evolution or the force of gravity; the shape of the face, the eyes, the features can change, but essentially what never changes is the overall physical conformation: two legs, two arms, a torso, and a head. This is because – it must be emphasized – the body has to be functional for the evolutive purpose of the individual. We should absolutely eliminate any idea, inspired by science fiction or the movies, of animal-like or simple shapes, since these would not have a development of limbs functional for the purposes of evolution and would not have permitted a civilization that hosts a conscience to experience and manifest all the necessary nuances of evolution. An animal's body, in a nutshell, furnishes only the tools necessary for the experiences pertaining to that type of evolution. A higher evolution necessarily requires a body suitable for its purpose.

Thus the experiences are analogous. *On certain planets the point of evolution can be inferior to your current one, and on others it*

---

[151] Florence Circle 77, *Maestro, perché?*, p. 102.
[152] *Ibid.*, pp. 185-186.

could be higher; the organizations, the societies may be different, and there are indeed some very nice things that I hope can be achieved also by human beings, while others correspond to your evolutionary past; however, the path traveled is similar.[153]

There are many, a great many, planets that host forms of life. Some are still in an early evolutionary period, one that pertains so to speak to our evolutionary past, to what is our history.

Others are going through the same evolutionary period as Earth today, and others still have already gone beyond the critical moment for every civilization which marks the definitive entrance into an evolved understanding of man and the cosmos, which is invariably followed by the possibility of access to specific dynamics of physics – which we are now just beginning to glimpse – that enable an evolved race to move about in space in the enormous distances where light does not reach.

Some civilizations are much more evolved than ours, both technologically and socially, and above all spiritually. *Other civilizations more prosperous than yours exist, from both the technological and spiritual viewpoints.*[154] These civilizations have already discovered the way to prolong life by several hundred years. This possibility is the natural consequence of the fact that, having achieved a certain level of evolution, the individual's ego is much freer of preconceptions, pressing desires, conditionings, and selfish thoughts, and acts more out of altruism than egotism.

Thus it doesn't make sense to renew the physical vehicle too early, since the same personality allows this individual to have many more experiences without remaining crystallized in the preconceptions and selfish desires typical of the average level of evolution on Earth. A person of today would remain blocked in his evolution for too long if he had now the possibility of living for hundreds of years. Currently there would be no use living for 300 years if his experiences were always filtered through the same self-centered personality, by the egotistical ego that would do nothing other than accumulate karma which would be onerous to work off. A civilization of this sort would never evolve, since it would be

---

[153] Florence Circle 77, ed. by V. Bilotta, *Dizionario del Cerchio Firenze 77*, Rome, Mediterranee, 1988, p. 23.
[154] Florence Circle 77, *Maestro, perché?*, p. 187.

governed for very long periods by the same people or by very similar mentalities.

Will we, too, manage to discover how to lengthen mankind's life expectancy?

In effect, in the future our civilization, too, could find something of the sort. But this can happen only when man has achieved an evolution such that he can be renewed in his inner self, above and beyond the renewal of the body. In other words, it is necessary that the renewal of the body be matched by a psychic renewal: otherwise, prolonging life would not serve any purpose.[155]

Prolonging human life – which would be the equivalent of granting the ego its dearest dream – without the enthusiasm of wanting to renew oneself every day, of helping oneself and society to evolve, would be completely useless.

Your Earth, as a term of comparison, can be considered a planet where the life of individuals faces mid-level difficulties. There are planets where life, as you conceive of it, has amply overcome all the material difficulties and deals only with difficulties of an intellectual and spiritual nature. Material difficulties – procuring food, earning a living, having to work to achieve a state of material wellbeing – no longer exist, because all this has been overcome.[156]

Is it possible to contact beings who are carrying out their evolution on other planets? Certainly it is possible, and it has already happened many times in the course of our history. Those who have experienced this contact are often saddened because others don't believe them. The fact is that these "contacts" have to remain personal experiences of the individuals who are directly involved and cannot yet become the common heritage of all mankind, if not on a level of knowledge and indirect information.

There exists a sublime law, according to which it is not permitted for one civilization to interfere with another, and we must thank the Most High for this, because it would mean depriving a civilization of its spiritual freedom. And this would make humankind the slave of other creatures; and in a plan of justice and impartiality, this would be absurd. We add that mankind would lose

---

[155] *Ibid.*

[156] Gruppo A7, *Nuovi messaggi dal mondo dello spirito*, Rome, Mediterranee, 1988, p. 62.

the taste, the love for seeking that has been the cause of the reawakening of the conscience of many creatures on your planet.[157]

Mankind would not evolve even one step if people did not achieve knowledge through all the intermediate steps that only direct experience can grant. It would be useless to give them knowledge of anti-gravitational propulsion, for instance, if they did not use it conscientiously, if they did not understand that behind aims of progress and discovery towards other worlds, in all probability, lurk egotistical aims of conquest and the exploitation of others' resources. And this is in the best of hypotheses; in the worst, man would turn his new technology against himself, using it as a weapon of power and command over other peoples of the Earth, other nations, as has already happened with nuclear energy.

What is the reason for the frequent visits from UFOs since World War II? Precisely to check on this use and abuse of nuclear energy.

The responsibility of limiting this technological knowledge has fallen to "observers" coming from other parts of this galaxy. They want to be in a position to be able to block any nuclear explosion that could threaten to set off a chain reaction of the type described.[158]

They fear that man could use atomic energy in an incautious and ignorant manner. The energy released by a nuclear reaction is so violent that it could literally cause a gash in the etheric matter, *like a rip in a cloth.*[159] If this hypothesis were to be realized, the etheric matter that makes up the physical plane would be sucked, as if in the vortex of a black hole, into the dimension immediately after it – in other words the elementary units would break apart and go back to being astral matter – with repercussions that would go beyond the balance of our solar system. *A similar event would result in the cancellation of all living matter in the galaxy.*[160] I am aware that what I just said could seem like a science fiction scene from some Hollywood movie. Here, as in the rest of this book, my aim is to make known information repeated numerous times and on different occasions by different sources that I consider reliable. The final

---

[157] Cerchio medianico Kappa, *Verso la scintilla*, Rome, Mediterranee, 1990, p. 92.
[158] Hilarion, *Threshold*, pp. 26-27.
[159] Hilarion, *The Nature of Reality*, p. 38.
[160] *Ibid.*

judgment lies within the logic and sensibility of each individual reader.

We have spoken of anti-gravitational propulsion. Now, without descending into a sterile science-fiction type description, the objection that often – and quite rightly, in terms of logic – is raised by scientists of our century is that the inhabitants of other planets, even if they had discovered a way of traveling through space at a speed, let us say, equal to that of light – the maximum velocity at which physical matter can travel, according to science – it would take these creatures hundreds or thousands of years before they could complete a one-way trip to Earth. Just as an example, the stellar mass of the Pleiades is "only" 440 light-years distant from our solar system.

So then, how can visiting extraterrestrials cover distances like this?

At the beginning of the journey towards Earth, the crews of the UFOs dematerialize themselves, along with their vehicles, transferring themselves into the astral plane. Then they rematerialize when they get close to Earth. Therefore their interplanetary trip is not physical but astral.

Only in this way, taking advantage of astral time, can they cover distances that, considered in the physical plane, would require an inconceivable time to be traversed.[161]

Increasing the vibration of the elementary unit beyond a certain threshold, it is as if matter disintegrated, even while managing to maintain the astral matrix – not etheric, which is still matter – then to be able to "rebuild" it once they have reached their destination. This is because a conscience that has reached a certain level of evolution, still attached to the mental and astral plane, will permit the reconstruction of the physical matrix.

In the astral mode, time, even though it exists, is not synchronized with material time; the distances in astral mode, we reiterate, are covered by means of the mere wish of the crew to arrive at a given point in space. Once at their destination, the vibrational field of the spaceship and its inhabitants enables it to "rebuild" the UFO, making it materialize close to Earth. In effect the spaceship, composed first only of astral matter, as its vibration

---

[161] Vitaliano Bilotta, *Evolvenza Serie Azzurra - Il canto della vita*, Rome, Cometa, 2011, p. 18 point 47.

slows becomes physical matter once again, definitively changing vibration and thus dimension. It is as if *the spiritual energy, left intact, made it possible to control the operation and complete it successfully. It is the absolute triumph of the spirit and of pure will over matter.*[162]

The system by which these flying objects reach Earth is – therefore *– a system of materialization-dematerialization-rematerialization close to the Earth's atmosphere.*[163]

Once it has rematerialized in the physical plane, the spaceship has no more need to move about in the astral and will move around in the Earth's atmosphere, not in the way our vehicles move by propulsion as we conceive of it, but literally "sliding" on the aether. This point is fundamental for understanding those sudden, almost unnatural, movements that UFOs make, which have by now become a part of narrative lore. Let's look at this in detail.

In normal propulsion the engine "pushes" the spaceship, which means that the engine causes an acceleration of the entire structure; consequently all the atoms that make it up are set in motion and accelerate, resulting in the forceful movement and sense of being crushed which the crew feels inside the cabin. The UFO's "engine" in reality does not effect any propulsion, but is based on the emission of *transversal* etheric vibrations that generate a gravity opposed to Earthly gravity (we shall discuss, in very simple terms, *transversal* vibrations of the elementary unit in the chapter devoted to gravity).

The anti-gravitational vibrations take place by means of the creation of an *etheric plasma*, the same that we have already seen for the sun and the cores of the planets; they result in two gravitational forces that oppose each other extremely violently, and the spaceship is pushed at a prodigious speed. In short, it is a sort of electromagnetic propulsion, if we wish to use the term closest to our scientific understanding, in which the spaceship is enveloped in a sort of "colored" cloud created by the electromagnetic field that is generated – the color of the *electromagnetic cloud* varies according to the intensity of the "propulsion," tending towards white at its highest speed – which allows it to move by *sliding* literally on the

---

[162] Delval Pierre, *Contatti del 4° tipo*, Milan, De Vecchi, 1979, p. 100.
[163] Florence Circle 77, *Maestro, perché?*, p. 196.

aether (the matrix of the physical plane).

The characteristic of this *sliding on the aether* does not result in the *progressive* acceleration or deceleration of the atoms that make up the spaceship, so that inside it no object or person feels any kind of thrust; the crew does not realize it is moving.

In other words: The gravitational field generated by the spaceship acts not only on each atom of the vehicle, but also on each atom that is inside it, including the passengers. Therefore, independently of the abrupt fluctuations of the spaceship, each particle within the influence of the gravitational field generated by the spaceship is in a *uniform state of acceleration*. Under these conditions, the acceleration has no effect either on the vehicle or on anything inside it.

All the spaceship's atoms are pushed along in unison. When the spaceship has to make a 90° turn or change direction by suddenly moving backwards, this happens without any internal movement and without the "flattening effect" typical of acceleration caused by conventional propulsion.

What is important to keep in mind, in the manifestation of these visitors, is that they never come with the aim of upsetting your civilization. This is very important: those who are farther along in evolution understand well that every civilization, every race has to have its own experiences in an autonomous manner.[164]

The inhabitants of other planets, who are so technologically evolved as to have discovered a way to traverse the immense distances that exist between the celestial bodies, are also highly evolved from the ethical and social points of view and know that they cannot interfere with the evolution of other forms of life.

We can set our minds at ease and not take into any consideration whatsoever those who claim to have the certainty of an imminent extraterrestrial landing on a planetary level. This awareness will arrive when mankind has achieved *naturally* the sufficient evolution which will enable people to live in a different mode from the exploitation of everything around them.

---

[164] *Ibid.*

Matter and vibration

Let us imagine we have the possibility of immersing ourselves into the world of the infinitely small and scrutinizing the origin of physical matter. Imagine we have a much keener organ of vision, so keen that it can see atoms one by one. The world that we are accustomed to seeing would no longer exist under this aspect: colors would no longer exist, or shapes; we could no longer distinguish if a material is solid or liquid. All matter, even our body, would not appear to us as anything other than a whirling and shaking of tiny, tiny particles, so numerous that we could no longer distinguish clearly between one shape of objects and another. The atoms of solid materials would be mixed in with the atoms of the air. We would still be able to detect, but not distinguish, the objects present in a room because we would see denser areas compared to less dense areas – corresponding to the air – where the atoms are present in a significantly inferior quantity than they are in the solids.

But let's take another step forward: imagine that you can see inside the atoms, all the way to the smallest particle, to the one we have called the *elementary unit*.

Having reached this point, our sight can no longer distinguish anything: we will have the vision exclusively of a sea of particles – like tiny balls – all uniform with each other. There will be no way of distinguishing them from each other: we will note only an enormous stretch of tiny balls identical and very close to each other. Even the enormous space present inside an atom, between the nucleus and an electron, will not really be empty but filled with these little balls. Cosmic space, too, between one planet and another, also apparently empty, will be filled with the same identical quantity of balls in every point. There does not exist, nor can there exist, any point that is truly empty: nothingness cannot exist. This is because, when all is said and done, it is the *elementary unit* that creates space, understood as a three-dimensional structure, as a matrix of the reality in which we live.

What official science calls "absolute void" does not really exist:

it is nothing more than an area in which the *elementary units* are in a condition of absolute rest. They do not move, they do not vibrate, they are immobile, but they are all there.

At this point we have glimpsed the first reality of the physical plane, the true form of its matter: that which, in the last analysis, makes up all of the physical plane. How can all these tiny balls identical to each other – the elementary units – create the ordinary matter that we know?

Let's imagine that something causes these balls to move. According to how they are moved, they start spinning or waving or vibrating. Every movement of one ball influences the ball next to it. They are all side by side, in such a way that there is no empty space between them. Every movement, therefore, of an elementary particle has effects on the particle next to it: the physical plane is nothing other than a sequence of causes and effects, a concept that recurs over and over both on the macrocosmic level and in the microcosm of a person's inner being.

Thus the waving movement of some elementary units will provoke, as a consequence of resonance,[165] the long propagation of a wave, like in the sea. Thus the vibrating of one particle will make all the particles around it vibrate too.

What happens if we now start making the space vibrate from multiple points? If we throw a rock into a calm pond, we will see the propagation of numerous overlapping waves, as in figure 8.

Fig. 8 – The waves generated by several stones interact with each other and, adding up, they generate waves increasingly complex

---

[165] Resonance is an "induced vibration": the rhythmic oscillations of a material provoke analogous oscillations in the material immediately adjacent to it, creating a synchronized wave having the same frequency.

The interference that one wave provokes on another in the physical plane is the beginning of what we could call the "generation of matter."

Physicists have already discovered that cosmic space, the void that exists between one celestial body and another, is "full of energy"[166]: it is a continuous creation and annihilation of infinitesimal, unstable particles that last only an instant, so small and rapid that they cannot be classified in their entirety by particle physics.

This light and constant "teeming" of energy and particles in the void is nothing other than the intersecting of multiple waves of elementary particles that, interacting with each other, now grouping together, now canceling each other out, produce what physics calls "interference."[167]

The waves, overlapping, generate a peak that grows to a maximum and then comes back down. According to intensity, in other words according to the "size" of that peak wave generated for an instant, we will have in the physical plane the rapid manifestation and annihilation of "energies" like light, gamma rays, or other forms of electromagnetic radiation.[168] This is the "energy of the void."

From this we can begin to understand that the word "energy" is nothing but the *effect* that the vibration of elementary units produces on the physical plane. In their interaction, in their "moving and shaking," the more elementary units are involved the more the energy on the physical plane will be evident, *to the point that it is possible to state that everything you see around you is nothing other*

---

[166] The "energy of the void" is a quantity of energy present everywhere in space even in the absence of matter, which makes the void a false void. The energy of the void can have measurable effects, including the spontaneous emission of light or gamma rays.

[167] In physics the phenomenon of interference is due to the superimposition, in one point in space, of two or more waves. What is observed is that the intensity (or breadth) of the resulting wave in that point can be different from the sum of the original intensities of the individual waves; in particular, this can vary from a minimum – where no wave phenomenon is observed – to a maximum coinciding with the sum of the intensities.

[168] "All the forms of electromagnetic radiation consist of photons: gamma rays, X rays, ultraviolet rays, light, infrared rays, radio waves, etc. Photons always travel at the speed of light (300.000 Km/sec) and have a resting mass of zero." James A. Haught, *Il vuoto di Torricelli*, Bari, Dedalo, 1996, p. 223.

than a different aggregation of these elementary particles from which, because of their greater or lesser aggregation, everything around you comes.[169]

Reasoning closely, it is not only the different aggregation of elementary units (from which the density of matter derives) that differentiates one object from another. This by itself is not sufficient to explain, for example, why ice and hot water have two temperatures very different from each other.

What, then, is it that elicits these different characteristics of the physical plane? It is the *vibration* of the elementary unit. I am not stating anything new from the standpoint of current science. This phenomenon is already well known.

What should be added, though, is that vibration produces different effects according to the level of aggregation of the matter: at the elementary unit level, a certain type of vibration will cause the effect of electromagnetic waves like light, for example. At the level of the atom, the vibration will have the effect of causing heat.

It seems clear that, in the last analysis, phenomena like light, sound, heat, electricity, magnetism, and radioactivity are nothing more than effects caused by different types of vibration of matter at smaller and smaller levels.[170]

To sum up:
- *the elementary unit* is the basic building block of the physical plane; the constituting element that creates the space and matter of our plane of existence and thus enables the structuring and organization of concrete reality around us;
- the elementary units all together form the *aether*, that is to say the matrix of the physical world;
- the physical plane is everywhere made up of the same identical element – the elementary unit – that *clumping together* with other elementary units forms particles, atoms, gases, liquids, and solids; in other words it forms all the reality of the physical plane and the various densities of matter;
- the *vibration* of elementary units is responsible for all the effects and characteristics of matter; it contributes to

---

[169] Ifior Circle, *Dall'Uno all'Uno*, vol. III, part I, p. 31.
[170] *Ibid.*, p. 45.

differentiating the physical phenomena that are perceived by our senses or by scientific instruments in the form of light, heat, electricity, and so on.

Now let's try to follow the path of this vibration from its first manifestation in an elementary unit until we reach the level perceived by our senses.[171]

The elementary unit vibrates, that is to say it moves, generating a wave of elementary units, which is propagated into the aether. If the wave encounters other waves (always generated by other elementary units that are vibrating in turn), like in a pond, the vibrations combine, interfering with each other and giving rise to an overall vibration different from the initial one.

We are at a very low level of density of matter, the simplest aggregation, the one that science has called "quantum" (such as photons, whose vibrations give rise, as effect, to phenomena like light, for example).

Bit by bit as the waves interfering with each other increase, ever more complex vibrations will result, which will summon an ever greater number of elementary units until "particles" are generated, from tiny neutrinos up to more massive aggregations like photons and neutrons. We have reached the "atomic nucleus."

The mechanism of creation of the mass of matter will be analyzed in detail in the next chapter.

What happens if we take apart the matter so constituted? What would happen is that an electron would go back to being undifferentiated matter: As it falls apart it would progressively lose its "energy," so that its moving and spinning would be transformed, like in a small explosion, into a movement of all the nearby elementary units, until the energy is totally dispersed, as in a wave. This is in a nutshell what happens in particle accelerators or when matter and antimatter are made to collide.

A particle, in the extreme hypothesis of annihilation, does not disappear from the physical plane but simply goes back to being an elementary unit in a state of rest, and as it loses its vibratory motion, instruments detect the residual vibrations as *energy*.

---

[171] *Ibid.*, p. 48.

The creation of matter and cymatics

Now let's try to understand how an initial "tangle" of vibrations can agglomerate a quantity of tiny, infinitesimal balls of elementary units big enough to generate a solid form, like the nucleus of an atom.

To understand the order of magnitude we are talking about, it is as though we gathered together many specks of dust and made them stick together until they formed a ball a kilometer in diameter, but without using any glue to hold them together!

Now let's take up again our discussion of the vibrations of elementary units, starting from the following example. Imagine a wire that, if it is moved at one end, begins vibrating as in figure 9.

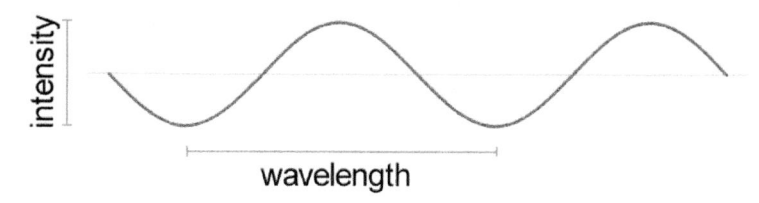

Fig. 9 – Vibration of a string made to oscillate with a periodic movement

The same thing happens when the elementary units are set in vibration, generating a wave like in the sea.

The elementary units vibrate horizontally with respect to the direction of propagation of the wave, like an "impact" of elementary units on the closest ones, as in a chain reaction. The "impact," or to put it better the progressive *compression and dilation* of the aether to form a wave, is the type of vibration of the physical plane that pertains to the diffusion of electromagnetic waves (light and photons in general). Now imagine putting another wave next to it, as in figure 10.

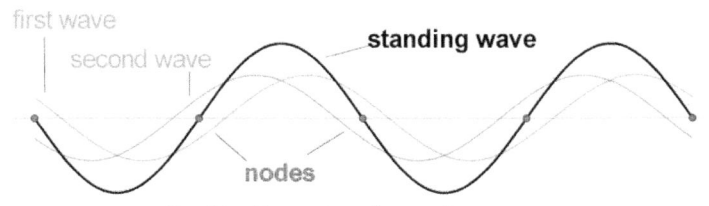

Fig. 10 – Formation of a standing wave

The first wave will move leftwards, the second towards the right. What is happening? It happens that a third wave is formed, called a *standing wave* (also known as a *stationary wave*), as the result of the sum of movement of the two. The characteristic of the standing wave is that there is no propagation along a certain direction in space like the two preceding ones; it will not go to the left or to the right, but will only oscillate up and down for the duration, remaining in the same position, unmoved. It will also happen that this standing wave will present points, called *nodes*, where the sum of the waves will always be zero. In fact, the standing wave will oscillate periodically up and down and in those *nodal points* the wave will always be null and immobile.

Now things start to get interesting. Observe the image in figure 11. As early as the beginning of the eighteenth century it was noticed that, if someone put powder on a membrane to form a uniform layer and activated a continuous vibration, precise geometric patterns were formed. The powder, subjected to the constant vibrations of the surface on which it is spread, tends to accumulate in the parts where the vibration at that point is nullified.

Fig. 11 – A generator of frequencies used to experiment with geometric figures obtained by vibrating a surface sprinkled with a fine dust (lycopodium powder, fine sand, or even ordinary flour)

It is as though the geometric figure created were a *three-dimensional standing wave*, in which the powder stops still in the zero point of the vibration, that is to say in the multitude of fixed points corresponding to the *nodal points*.

Now imagine that the specks of powder on the vibrating membrane are elementary units, and suppose that the particles are forced to vibrate in a three-dimensional space such as is our physical reality; we deduce that from a vibration of this sort we can obtain a geometric figure fully resembling a *three-dimensional solid*, varying in complexity according to the multiplicity of the vibratory frequencies of the elementary units involved.

Even if this example is simplistic, it is feasible, by means of simple vibration, to give form and volume to the various physical particles and, progressively as the vibrations overlap, generate more and more complex figures: aggregation by aggregation, we arrive at the protons and neutrons of an atomic nucleus[172]; and with the repetition of the same mechanism we achieve the formation of all the atoms of the periodic table of elements.[173]

Returning to the geometric structures, we can admire the evocative images taken from the work done by Hans Jenny and the research engineers Weiyu Ran and Steven Fredericks of Clemson University[174] (fig. 12).

---

[172] In reality, before arriving at protons and neutrons, the elementary units aggregate in particles known today as quarks. We know from physics that every proton and every neutron is made up of three quarks each. The quarks take shape at the same moment as the "creation" of the proton and neutron. Quarks are unstable and only last an instant, since at the moment of the breakdown of a proton or neutron their spin is unbalanced and partial before they go back to being sub-quarks and then undifferentiated matter (elementary unit). It is worth noting David G. Yurth's comment that already in 1990 a good 450 scientists confirmed the existence of sub-quarks.

[173] The physicist Stephen M. Phillips, in his two books *Extrasensory Perception of Quarks* of 1980 and *ESP of Quarks and Superstrings* of 1999, gave rigorous scientific proof of the fact that the mediums Besant and Leadbeater had communicated as early as 1895 the quantum nature of physical matter, quarks and sub-quarks even into the most minute detail, long before the official scientific discovery! (See Besant A. & Leadbeater C.W., *Occult Chemistry*, London, A. P. Sinnett, 1895).

[174] See W. Ran and S. Fredericks, *Shape oscillation of a levitated drop in an acoustic field*, Clemson University, *YouTube* video.

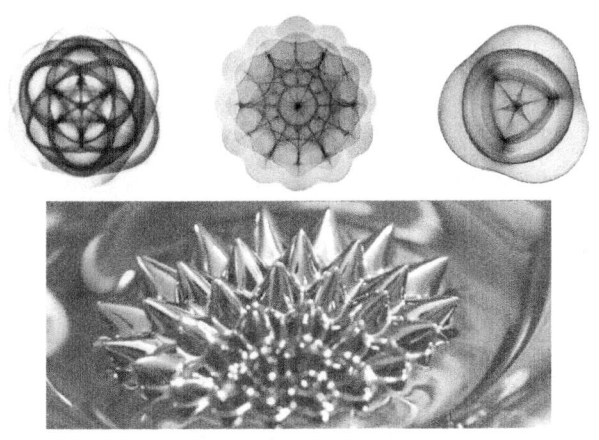

Fig. 12 – Two- and three-dimensional images obtained during cymatics experiments

In the past few decades the study of these figures has been taken up by cymatics (from the Greek *kymatika*, which means the "study of waves").

In 1967 the Swiss physician Hans Jenny, considered the father of cymatics, published the first of two volumes titled *Kymatic*, in which – drawing inspiration from the experiences of the German physicist Ernst Chladni on the effects of vibrations – he maintained the existence of a subtle power by means of which sound gives structure to matter.

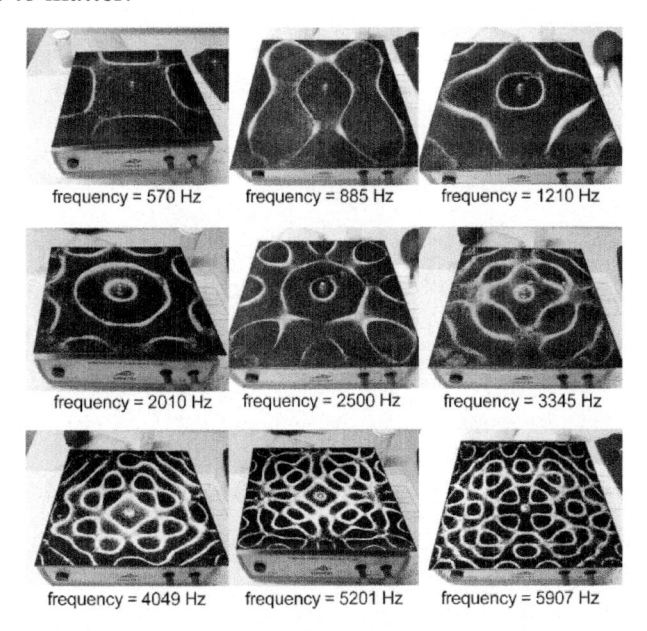

Fig. 13 – Each frequency is matched by a three-dimensional image in the sand on the moving membrane

139

In his experiments he placed sand on a metal plate connected to a sound oscillator which produced a broad spectrum of frequencies. The sand organized itself into various structures characterized by geometric shapes that were all different and more complex according to the frequency (i.e., the vibration) emitted by the oscillator. Pythagoras, already in his time, intuited and maintained that "the geometry of forms is solidified music."

Figure 15 shows some "vibrating strings," postulated by modern physics in "string theory," as constituting the basis of matter. Their resemblance to the geometries created by cymatics confirms this theory.

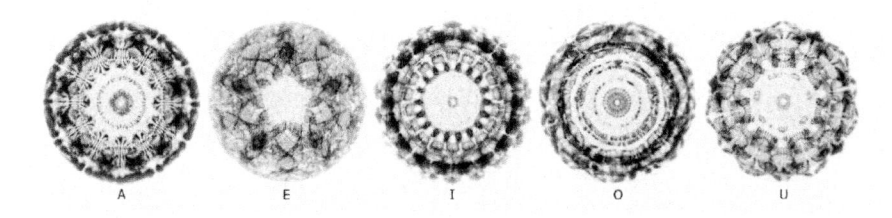

Fig. 14 – Geometric shapes corresponding to the sounds emitted by human vowels

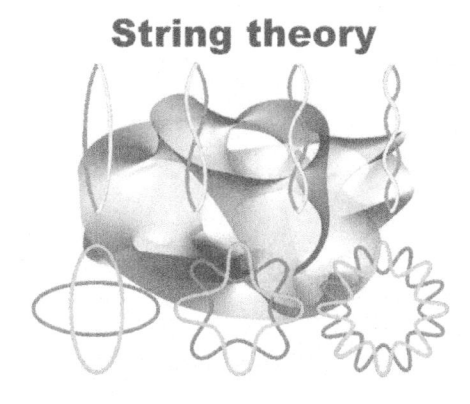

Fig. 15 – Representation of the strings postulated by "string theory"

Gravity

From the beginning, the force of gravity has been the object of confusion. What man observes of nature is always the external manifestation of what appears in intrinsic reality, and he does this from a point of view consonant with his possibilities of perception, even when carried out with the most scrupulous and scientific observation.

Gravity is a shining example. Observing nature, the obvious and immediate deduction that an observer can make is that it consists of a force of *attraction* between two bodies. In reality, precisely the opposite is true. Gravity is a *push*.

Let's try to understand what is meant by gravitational "push," taking the simple example of the miniscule little balls seen in the chapter on matter. Imagine a space full of tiny balls, all squeezed next to each other, compressed. If in one point of this space we create a "hole," in correspondence with that hole a depression will be created, that is to say, the little balls pushing on each other will tend to close the hole; thus they will exercise a thrust towards the hole. Imagine that we are standing on the outer edge of that hole. We would have the sensation of being pushed towards the center of the hole, but from our point of view, not seeing anything else, it will seem to us that we are being "attracted" towards the center (fig. 16).

If there were two holes, as in figure 17, the push, besides acting on both in each point, would act with lesser intensity in the area where the two holes cast shadows on each other, resulting in the appearance that the two "holes" are moving closer to each other. In other words, it will look like the bodies are attracting each other.

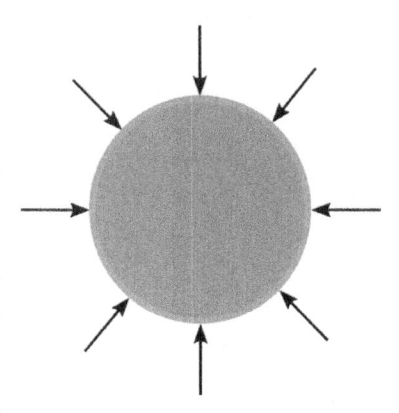

Fig. 16 – Thrust exercised by the balls around the hole

141

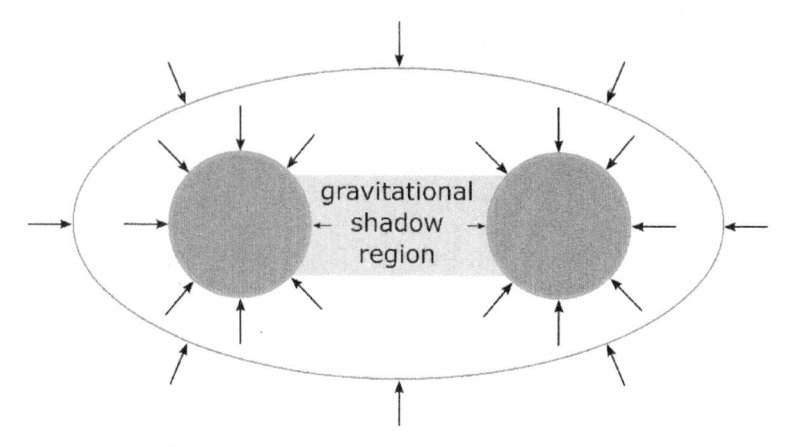

Fig. 17 – Simplified illustration of gravity as a force of thrust that acts on two celestial objects, resulting in a gravitational pull of one celestial body on the other

Space, the plane of matter, is completely pervaded and immersed in a matrix, a sort of very dense grid of elementary units. This is the etheric matrix, or more simply *aether*.

The concept of gravity as a push, just like the existence of the aether in place of the void, is not a recent intuition.

Descartes explained the solar system as a gigantic etheric vortex, like a whirlwind, in which the planets are immersed. Fresnel explained the wave nature of light as a vibrating of that medium, as a fluid (the aether), and later Herz demonstrated that the concept of electromagnetism arose thanks to the hypothesis that space was full of a medium vibrating like a fluid, called aether. Guglielmo Marconi later applied this concept by imagining it as functional for the wireless telegraph. All the discoveries of the past were made postulating the existence of the aether.

On the postulate of the aether, the inventor Georges-Louis Le Sage in 1743 was the first to hypothesize that gravity thus acted by pushing.[175]

---

[175] In his essay on the "Theory of Gravity" in 1743 and later in 1747, Le Sage wrote: "Eureka, Eureka. I have never had a greater satisfaction than in this moment, when I have just explained rigorously, from the simple law of movement in a straight line, those of universal gravity, which diminishes in the same proportion as the square of the distance" (See Matthew R. Edwards, *Pushing Gravity: New Perspectives on Le Sage's Theory of Gravitation*, Montreal,

In 1903, it was the Italian physicist Olinto De Pretto's turn to repropose the thesis of the origin of gravity as a force of thrust.[176]

Isaac Newton, too, in his more "mature" return to the subject almost twenty years after his "law of universal gravitation," wrote in *Opticks* a reconsideration of gravity as a thrust, not an attraction. Here it is:

> Is not this Medium much rarer within the dense Bodies of the Sun, Stars, Planets and Comets, than in the empty Celestial spaces between them? ... For if this Medium be rarer within the Sun's Body than at its Surface... it may suffice to impel Bodies from the denser parts of the Medium towards the rarer, with all that power which we call Gravity.[177]

We must now clarify better what we mean by "thrust" (or push).

Looking more closely, the "thrust" that we detect in our physical plane is in reality a wave that is propagated in the astral plane but has tangible effects in the physical plane as gravity. It is a vibratory wave that we could call *transversal*, in the sense that the vibration is propagated orthogonally, i.e., perpendicular with respect to the physical plane. The elementary unit is not "pushed" by the elementary units next to it, as in the case of electromagnetic waves; that is to say, there is not the sort of "impact" that is propagated from one elementary unit to another generating a vibratory wave.

The example in figure 18 helps us understand gravity. Imagine that the arrow is the transversal vibration. The elementary unit vibrates in a direction perpendicular to the physical plane. It is like when we pull a stretched-out cloth downwards and note that a depression is formed. So then gravity is in reality a "curvature" of the physical plane caused by the vibratory force that "pulls" the aether transversally.

Apeiron, 2002, pp. 9-40).

[176] See Olinto De Pretto, *Ipotesi dell'Etere nella Vita dell'Universo* [Atti del Reale Istituto Veneto di Scienze, Lettere ed Arti, Anno Accademico 1903-1904, vol. LXIII, part II, pp. 439-500].

[177] Isaac Newton, *Opticks, or a Treatise of the Reflections, Refractions, Inflections and Colours of Light*, New York, Dover Publications Inc., 1952, Book III, part I, question 21, pp. 350-351 (http://strangebeautiful.com/other-texts/newton-opticks-4ed.pdf).

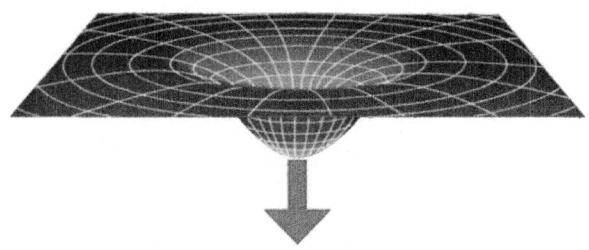

Fig. 18 – Gravity is in reality not a force, but the "curvature" of the physical plane caused by the transversal vibration of the elementary unit

This depression, propagating itself throughout all the space occupied by a planet, would result, in the physical dimension, in the effect of a "push." This is the greatest simplification we can do.

The "push" of space is a concept much more adaptable to Einstein's space-time curvature than to Newton's attraction. In fact, if for Le Sage and De Pretto it is space that "pushes" masses, for Einstein it is space-time that "guides" masses towards the center of gravity (fig. 19). This latter statement is the more correct of the two: the "push," if we want to call it that, is guided by the dimension immediately after the physical one: the *astral dimension*.

Even if the concept is very similar, we could call it the "space-astral" curvature, since it is not time but space that curves towards the dimension just below: the astral one.

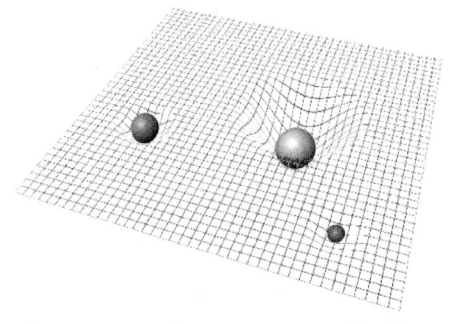

Fig. 19 – The "space-time" curvature posited by Einstein which "guides", as a result, the mass towards the gravitational center

In essence, in the planets and the sun, what sets off the transversal vibration of gravity? Once again the etheric plasma! It is the etheric plasma of the sun, the Earth, and all the other celestial bodies that causes the *transversal* vibration of the elementary units contained in the plasma and the resulting gravitational effect, the "push" from the center of the plasma outwards.

We could even have stopped here with our explanation of the phenomenon of gravity. But the most attentive readers at this point will have noticed an incongruence: if it is etheric plasma that causes the "push" outwards, how do we reconcile the concept of gravity with the fact that the center of the Earth *pushes* and the sun also *pushes*? If also the core of our planet *pushes* instead of attracting, how is gravity formed on the Earth's crust?

Let's look at figure 20. The plasma core in the center of the Earth pushes from inside outwards, towards space, and this thrust diminishes as we move away from the center. At a certain point the gravitational thrust will begin progressively to lose strength compared to the thrust of the surrounding aether, until it reaches a point in which the thrust of the plasma will be equal to the thrust of the external aether. What will be the result? A point of equilibrium in which the two forces of thrust are equal to each other.

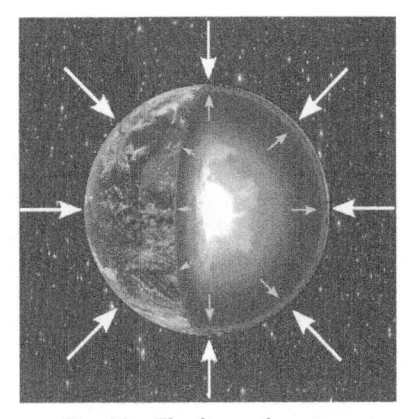

Fig. 20 – The force of gravity on Earth is formed as a result of the balance achieved between the lesser internal thrust of plasma and the greater external thrust of the cosmos.

Remember the other characteristic we mentioned about etheric plasma: it creates new matter, that is to say it brings new elementary units, taking them from the astral plane. So then, like a little sun, etheric plasma creates new matter and pushes it, literally, outwards towards the surrounding space; the new matter will travel until it stops where there is a point of equilibrium between the two thrusts. The matter created will all converge into the layer surrounding the point of equilibrium, slowly creating what is the Earth's crust.

In broad outlines, we are describing the formation of a planet. Over time the shell of matter will grow larger and thicker, it will expand and begin to become more rarefied in the layers of the outer crust, to grow dense into solid matter and crystallize into rock. Thus we reconnect with the theory of "expansion tectonics."

And this is how the growth of the Earth's gravity is explained. Figure 21 supports us in our explanation. When the Earth was smaller, the internal thrust was stronger, since the crust was closer to the core. As it grew larger, the crust also moved farther away from the core of plasma – which stayed the same size – and this allowed the external thrust to prevail over the internal one, with the result that gravity increased.

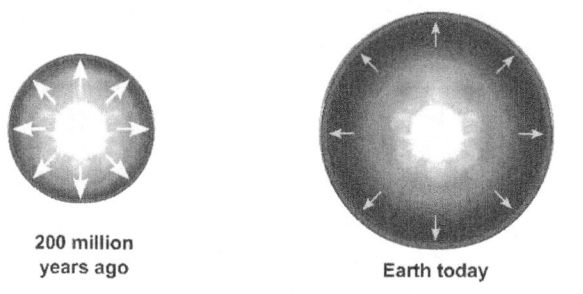

200 million years ago　　　　**Earth today**

Fig. 21 – The external thrust is stronger in a larger Earth, since the core is farther away from the crust. The result is a greater force of gravity compared to the Earth when it was smaller

Looking more closely, the sun also undergoes the same process: the outer shell that we see on the sun is the film formed at the point of equilibrium between the internal push of the plasma and the pressure exercised by the surrounding aether. In that point the two forces of thrust are equal, forming the film of extremely hot matter that we can all admire.

The enormous size of the sun in any case prevents the accumulation of a crust on its surface, except for the thin visible film. The thrust that comes from inside – with respect to the external thrust of the cosmos – enables the propagation in space of a great quantity of elementary units in vibration in the form of electromagnetic waves and particles.

Electricity and magnetism

In this last chapter I express my own personal, innovative reworking of what we have learned from official science and the theories transmitted by numerous Guides that have communicated with various spiritual circles.

Magnetism is a fairly simple concept. Maxwell,[178] Faraday,[179] Marconi,[180] and many others made their discoveries with the assumption that magnetism was a flow of aether. Let's try to understand better by drawing on alternative concepts of physics.

Magnetism is simply defined as *a current inside the aether*, a compact movement of elementary units *from one point to another*.[181] A flow of aether, as we just said. The best simile that comes to mind is the movement of a fluid, like a current of water.

The most immediate source from which we can deduce a movement of aether is the magnet, where the magnetic flow that is formed is a whirling flow of aether from north to south. That is, lines of force are generated that emerge from the magnet's north pole and enter into its south pole (fig. 22).

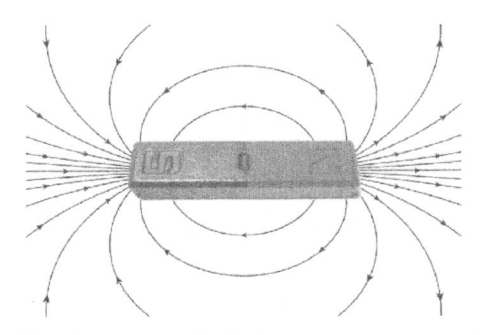

Fig. 22 – A magnet is a body that generates a magnetic field

---

[178] See J.C. Maxwell, *A Dynamical Theory of the Electromagnetic Field*, 1864.
[179] See M. Faraday, *Physical lines of magnetic forces*, Proc. of R. Ins., 1845.
[180] See Filippo Pacelli, *La conquista dell'etere. Il genio di Guglielmo Marconi. La guida di Temistocle Clazecchi-Onesti,* Florence, L'Autore Libri, 2009.
[181] Hilarion, *The Nature of Reality*, p. 28.

Another source of movement of aether is the flow of electrons through a conductor as a result of a current passing through it. With the help of some images, understanding of this mechanism will be immediate.

It is possible to imagine the electron as a vortex of aether spinning around itself. If we observed it with a powerful microscope we would see something like a little sphere revolving around itself. It is as if a great quantity of elementary units spun around, assuming the geometric shape of a *toroid* (a curve parallel to an ellipse, see fig. 23). In nature electron always spins in the same direction, and the negative charge is given by this direction of rotation.[182]

When it is set moving along a conductor, the electron always tends to orient itself in the same direction as the flow of movement. To give a figurative example, it is as though the electron entered the conductor channel always "from the top."

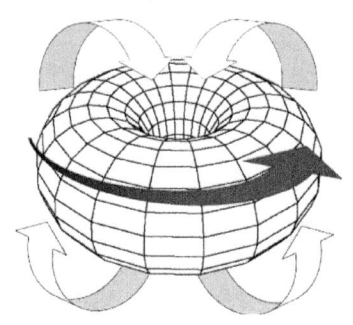

Fig. 23 – The electron is like a toroidal vortex of elementary units

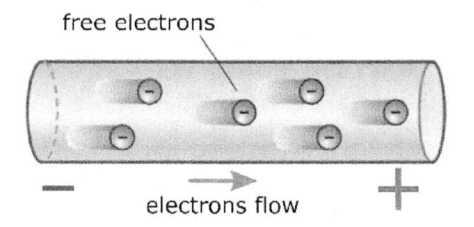

Fig. 24 – The flow of electrons in a metallic conductor is an orderly movement of particles all spinning in the same direction

---

[182] A particle's charge is given by the direction of its spin. A proton, too, spins around itself, but in the opposite direction from the electron. Antimatter is nothing more than the same particle spinning in the opposite direction. Thus, when it collides with a positron – an electron with a positive charge – they will annihilate each other because of their opposite spins, transferring their residual energy to the adjoining elementary units, in other words putting them in a momentary state of vibration that scientific instruments will detect as photons or other particles. Their matter is not annihilated, but electron and positron will simply go back to being elementary units in a different state of vibration.

Let's look at figure 24. All the electrons that run along the electrical wire will do so always in the same direction, and they will all rotate in the same direction. This means that it is not the movement of the electrons of the conductor that generates magnetism, but their spinning in synchronization that generates it, since the electrons of the conductor do not move haphazardly but travel along and rotate all in the same alignment. It is as though the rotating in unison generated a big vortex around them. Thus the movement of the electrons generates an electrical current, and the vortex generates magnetism. The magnetic field would be generated just the same even if the electrons were still, since the multitude of electrons, spinning in synchronization, would cause a wide vortex of aether perpendicular to the conductor, that is to say not in the direction of the electrical wire but in the external part and all around the conductor. *It is this rotary movement of the aether that is perceived as a magnetic field around the conductor.*[183] Then, in addition to spinning around the conductor, the aether will also travel along the entire conductor because at the same time the electron will move inside the conductor. In short: the flow of electrons inside the conductor generates electricity, the movement of the aether outside the conductor generates a magnetic field. From this we can understand why:

- when we speak of electricity we are also always talking about magnetism (electromagnetism);
- electromagnetic waves are transversal waves: the electrical field and the magnetic field, besides being at right angles to each other, are always perpendicular also to the direction of propagation, as illustrated in figure 25.

---

[183] Hilarion, *The Nature of Reality*, p. 28.

Propagation of an Electromagnetic Wave

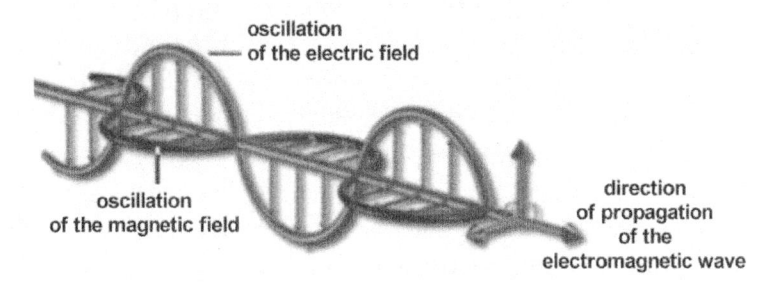

Fig. 25 – The magnetic field is at right angles to the electrical field

Observing the conductor in figure 24, while the direction of the current is propagated *horizontally*, the flow of aether (i.e., the magnetic field) spreads *vertically*, i.e., at right angles (perpendicular) to the current, widening out from the center of the conductor to beyond the outer edges.

This new vision of reality enables us also to understand readily why it is easy to reproduce the effect of a magnet by using electricity, as in an electromagnet. When a conducting wire is wrapped numerous times around a ferromagnetic core to form a coil, an enormous etheric vortex is formed, so big that it induces the iron core to orient and align its atoms – and thus its electrons – all in the same direction, which results in a relative magnetic field around the core, simulating the behavior of a magnet, as in figure 26.

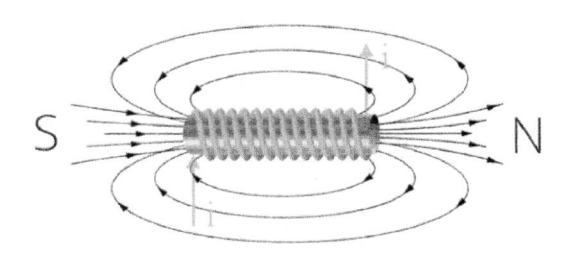

Fig. 26 – An electromagnet is made up of a nucleus of ferromagnetic material (usually "soft" iron) around which is wound a solenoid, i.e., a bobbin of many coils of electrical wire. When an electrical current runs through the wire, it transforms the bobbin into a magnet, in other words an etheric vortex.

Conclusion

Concluding this long journey of exploration of what moves us and surrounds us, I leave you with the words of the Guides, in the hope that the topics dealt with up to now can take on their proper meaning when these words are well understood and *felt* to be true, not by faith but because, through logic, they succeed in their intent to explain reality better than any religion or philosophy; and always when our conscience manifests dissatisfaction towards what current knowledge has to offer.

Enjoy reading.

Don't make what we say an issue of culture.

To be sure, culture is useful too, and can help with the exercise of logic, but often it shows itself to be a heavy chain on those who possess it, because it ends up becoming not a means for understanding more organically but an end to be achieved, maybe to feed and satisfy the desire of our ego to feel itself to be a step above the others, wrapping itself in "I know," which would be exhilarating if it were not for the fact that such unwarranted presumptuousness always brings sorrow.

There are countless incarnated persons, of humble origins and devoid of any type of cultural notion, who nonetheless feel and acquiesce to the logic of Reality better than learned scientists or illustrious personages renowned for their culture.

This does not mean disregarding what one knows and behaving with assumed humility, but being capable of drawing the essence from the reality one faces, without masking it under an avalanche of adornments that make comprehension and communication more difficult.

Because – and this is the last thing I want to tell you, children – remember that one who has understood a Truth, no matter how small, has the responsibility to preserve it intact and to suggest it – never imposing it – to the creatures who have not yet reached it but are headed in that direction.[184]

Ifior Circle

We close with the hope that we have contributed to bringing you to the threshold of a different conception of Reality. A new horizon is opening up before your eyes, a horizon that can be penetrated only by someone who has transcended the limits of human cognition. If we have succeeded, then this is not a farewell, but a welcome among those who are seeking the Reality that lies beyond what appears to us. The means to achieve this have been given to you: now it falls to you to bring about your inner transformation, which, once realized, is the only true revolution capable of changing the society in which you live.

Now it falls to you to give the proper value to the world in which you live, to love your neighbor by beginning to help those around you even more, and to acquire a sense of duty not understood as blind obedience but as a responsible sense of what humankind, in the highest sense of the word, is called to accomplish: to become who you are meant to be. From what we have said, it is clear that love of neighbor and the lofty teachings of morality have a logical explanation even more than a mystical inspiration. It cannot avoid helping you understand that the only apparent difference among people is the one deriving from their different phase of evolution. But even this difference cannot be interpreted in terms of "superior" or "inferior," but as the logical succession of many states of consciousness, of different ways of "feeling." The explanation of the real brotherhood among human beings cannot help leading you to view others with the greatest respect, whatever their condition, because they are creatures who are carrying out their experiences as each one does his own. From this it emerges that it makes no sense to hate someone who makes you suffer

---

[184] Ifior Circle, *Dall'Uno all'Uno,* vol. IV, pp. 21-22.

because these people – above and beyond their intent, which will have repercussions on their future lives – are nothing more than channels through which each person reaps what he has sown. It illustrates how, above and beyond the chaos and apparent randomness, everything is perfectly ordered, even while leaving each person a margin of individual freedom which is larger or smaller in relation to the breadth of conscience achieved. The conviction that Reality is structured in this way cannot avoid giving us a sense of tranquility, serenity, and confidence that the destiny of every being is the achievement of a state of conscience that is fully complete, above and beyond pleasure and pain, love and hate, good and evil, knowledge and ignorance.

May peace be with you and all of mankind. [185]

Florence Circle 77

---

[185] Florence Circle 77, *Oltre l'illusione*, pp. 294-295.

Acknowledgements

Special thanks go to my wife Irene, who for all these years has been friend, support, and inspiration.

I dedicate this book to her, the unwitting mentor of my evolutionary path. But above all, I thank her for giving me Samuele, my son. In the modest sphere of one's life, children expand one's mind. And they do this in the same measure as the responsibility they bring with them.

When we thank, inevitably we charge our words with our emotions: to you, my two true loves, I dedicate my time.

Because if it is true that evolution is individual, it is equally true that we need each other in order to evolve.

Bibliography and photo credits

Besant A. and Leadbeater C.W.: *Occult Chemistry*, London, A. P. Sinnett, 1895.
Bilotta, Vitaliano: *Evolvenza Serie Azzurra - Il canto della vita*, Rome, Cometa, 2011.
Cerchio Firenze 77, ed. by V. Bilotta: *Dizionario del Cerchio Firenze 77*, Rome, Mediterranee, 1988.
Cerchio Firenze 77: *Conosci te stesso?*, Rome, Mediterranee, 1990.
Cerchio Firenze 77: *Dai mondi invisibili*, Rome, Mediterranee, 1977.
Cerchio Firenze 77: *La fonte preziosa*, Rome, Mediterranee, 1987.
Cerchio Firenze 77: *La voce dell'ignoto*, Rome, Mediterranee, 1983.
Cerchio Firenze 77: *Le Grandi verità ricercate dall'uomo*, Rome, Mediterranee, 1982.
Cerchio Firenze 77: *Maestro, perché?*, Rome, Mediterranee, 1985.
Cerchio Firenze 77: *Oltre l'illusione*, Rome, Mediterranee, 1978.
Cerchio Firenze 77: *Per un mondo migliore*, Rome, Mediterranee, 1981.
Cerchio Ifior: *Dall'Uno all'Uno*, Genoa, Ins-Edit, 2009-2014, voll. I-IV
Cerchio Ifior: *La crisalide*, Genoa, Ins-Edit, 1991.
Cerchio Ifior: *Morire e vivere*, Genoa, Ins-Edit, 1992.
Cerchio Ifior: *Sussurri nel vento*, Genoa, Ins-Edit, 1991.
Cerchio medianico Kappa: *Verso la scintilla*, Rome, Mediterranee, 1990.
Chernet, Brook T. and Levin, Michael: "Transmembrane voltage potential is an essential cellular parameter for the detection and control of tumor development in a Xenopus model," *Disease Models & Mechanisms*, 2013 (http://dmm.biologists.org/content/6/3/595).
Conselice, Christopher J., A. Wilkinson, K. Duncan, A. Mortlock, University of Nottingham UK: "The evolution of galaxy number density at $z < 8$ and its implications," *The Astrophysical Journal*, October 2016.
De Pretto, Olinto: *Ipotesi dell'Etere nella Vita dell'Universo* [Atti del Reale Istituto Veneto di Scienze, Lettere ed Arti, Anno Accademico 1903-1904, vol. LXIII, parte II].
Delval, Pierre: *Contatti del 4° tipo*, Milan, De Vecchi, 1979.
Dembech, Giuditta: *L'ultimo Tabù*, Turin, Ariete Multimedia, 2009.
Emerson, Ralph Waldo: *The Conduct of Life*, Boston, Fireside Editions, 1909.
Faraday, M.: *Physical Lines of Magnetic Forces*, 1845.
Frank, A. and W.T. Sullivan: "A New Empirical Constraint on the Prevalence of Technological Species in the Universe," *Astrobiology Journal*, May 2016, New York, Mary Ann Liebert, Inc., publishers, 2016.
Gruppo A7: *Nuovi messaggi dal mondo dello spirito*, Rome, Mediterranee, 1988.
Haught, James A.: *Il vuoto di Torricelli*, Bari, Dedalo, 1996.
Hilarion: *The Nature of Reality*, Spigno Saturnia (LT), Crisalide, 1997.
Hilarion: *Seasons of the Spirit*, Spigno Saturnia (LT), Crisalide, 1992.
Hilarion: *Threshold*, Spigno Saturnia (LT), Crisalide, 1992.
Holden, Theodore Albon: *Dinosaurs, Gravity, and Changing Scientific Paradigms*, Bear Fabrique, 2004 (http://www.bearfabrique.org/FBook_Utube_Materials/gravity_PastAges.pdf).
Keinan, A. and A.G. Clark: "Recent Explosive Human Population Growth Has Resulted in an Excess of Rare Genetic Variants," *Science*, 2012, vol. 336, Issue 6082.
Leibniz, Gottfried Wilhelm Von: *Theodicy: Essays on the Goodness of God, the Freedom on Man and the Origin of Evil*. Translated by E. M. Huggard. La Salle, IL, Open Court, 1985.
Magister: *Voci lontane, vicine presenze*, Cornaredo (MI), Armenia, 2001.

Mantovani, Roberto: "Le fratture della crosta terrestre e la teoria di Laplace," *Bull. Soc. Sc. et Arts Réunion*, 1889.
Maxlow, James: "Expansion Tectonics" and "Magnetic Seafloor Mapping" (http://www.jamesmaxlow.com).
Maxwell, J. C.: A *Dynamical Theory of the Electromagnetic Field*, 1864.
Moody, Raymond A.: *Life After Life*, San Francisco, HarperSanFrancisco, 2001.
Moravia, Sergio: *Filosofia*, Florence, Le Monnier, 1999.
Newton Isaac: *Opticks, or a Treatise of the Reflections, Refractions, Inflections and Colours of Light*, New York, Dover Publications Inc., 1952 (http://strangebeautiful.com/other-texts/newton-opticks-4ed.pdf).
Norton L., R.M. Gibson, T. Gofton, C. Benson, S. Dhanani, S.D. Shemie, L. Hornby, R. Ward, and G.B. Young, University of Western Ontario in Canada: *Electroencephalographic recordings during withdrawal of life-sustaining therapy until 30 minutes after declaration of death* (https://www.ncbi.nlm.nih.gov/pubmed/28231862).
Pacelli, Filippo: *La conquista dell'etere. Il genio di Guglielmo Marconi. La guida di Temistocle Clazecchi-Onesti*, Florence, L'Autore Libri, 2009.
Pennetta: "Neodarwinismo alla 'deriva': la speciazione allopatrica conduce all'estinzione", *Critica Scientifica*, May 2012.
Plato: *Phaedo*, LVIII.
Ran, W. and S. Fredericks: *Shape oscillation of a levitated drop in an acoustic field*, Clemson University, YouTube video.
Sacco, Laurent: "Les dinosaures étaient moins massifs qu'on ne le pensait," *Futura Planète*, 3/7/2009.
Schopenhauer, Arthur: *On the Freedom of the Will*, translated by Eric J. Payne, Cambridge, Cambridge University Press, 1999.
Sensi, Ennio: *La vita nei livelli astrali*, Rome, Hermes, 1989.
Thompson, Bert: *The Origin Of Species and Darwin's Reference to "the Creator,"* Montgomery, Apologetics Press, 2003.
Vella, Luciano: *Enciclopedia Medica Italiana*. Aggiornamento II Edizione. Florence, USES Edizioni Scientifiche, 1993.
Voldben, Amadeus. *La Reincarnazione*, Rome, Mediterranee, 1999.
Yarkovsky Osipovich, Ivan, *Ipotesi cinetica della Gravitazione universale e connessione con la formazione degli elementi chimici*, 1888.

Photo credits

The images that illustrate this book were duly acquired from the following:

- cymascope.com: *fig. 14*
- ESA.int: *fig. 19*
- GoGraph: *fig. 1*
- jamesmaxlow.com: *figs. 3 and 4*
- NASA.gov: *fig. 7*
- Wikimedia Commons: *figs. 2, 5, 8, 11, 18, 26*
- Wikipedia: *figs. 6, 12, 13, 22, 25*
- All others not listed above were taken by the author.

Printed in Great Britain
by Amazon